"Well-written, logical, and easy to follow, *Successful Problem Solving* takes the mystery out of moving from hopeless frustration to workable solutions. The first self-help book to teach readers not only how to solve problems, but also how to modify dysfunctional beliefs that interfere with effective problem-solving.

> —Thomas E. Ellis, Psy.D., ABPP, Retired Professor of Psychology, West Virginia University School of Medicine, and author, *Choosing to Live: How to Defeat Suicide through Cognitive Therapy*

"This book provides one of the clearest descriptions of how to use cognitive strategies to change longstanding, negative core beliefs, and provides detailed suggestions for overcoming emotional blocks to solving problems effectively. If negative emotions such as fear, anxiety, depression, and anger keep getting in the way, the exercises in this book will help. I recommend it highly."

> —Martin M. Antony, Ph.D., Director, Anxiety Treatment and Research Centre, St. Joseph's Healthcare, Associate Professor, Psychiatry and Behavioral Neurosciences, McMaster University, and author of *When Perfect Isn't Good Enough* and *The Shyness and Social Anxiety Workbook*

"Living life means solving problems. Of course there are some problems that get in the way of solving problems. Organized, upbeat, and scientifically grounded, McKay and Fanning help readers become better equipped to make effective decisions and important changes in their lives. After all, problems worth solving are worth solving well."

> —Thomas F. Cash, Ph.D., Professor of Psychology, Old Dominion University and author, *The Body Image Workbook*

SUCCESSFUL PROBLEM SOLVING

A Workbook to Overcome the
Four Core Beliefs That Keep You Stuck

MATTHEW McKAY, PH.D.
PATRICK FANNING

Distributed in the U.S.A. by Publishers Group West; in Canada by Raincoast Books; in Great Britain by Hi Marketing, Ltd.; in South Africa by Real Books, Ltd.; in Australia by Boobook; and in New Zealand by Tandem Press.

Copyright © 2002 by Matthew McKay and Patrick Fanning
New Harbinger Publications, Inc.
5674 Shattuck Avenue
Oakland, CA 94609

Cover design by Poulson/Gluck
Edited by Brady Kahn
Text design by Tracy Powell-Carlson

ISBN 1-57224-302-3 Paperback

New Harbinger Publications' Web site address: www.newharbinger.com

04   03   02

10   9   8   7   6   5   4   3   2   1

First printing

For Peter D. Rogers, Ph.D., much loved friend, trusted colleague.
        —M.M.

For my son, Michael
        —P.F.

Contents

Part 2
Problem Solving

Part 1

Changing Your Core Beliefs

1

First Things First: Getting at the Source of What Keeps You Stuck

Life is one long series of problems. That's the bad news. The good news is that most of them can be solved. The method you'll learn in this book works. If you complete the five simple steps—Assessment, Brainstorming, Consequences, Do List, and Evaluation—we guarantee you'll make significant progress toward solving any problem. That doesn't mean everything will be perfect. Just better.

The types of problems we'll look at here focus on:

- Emotions

- Relationships

- Work/Career

- Education/Knowledge

- Money

- Recreation/Pleasure

- Environment

- Health

No matter how long or unsuccessfully you've worked on difficulties in any of these arenas, we'll show you a way to make positive changes.

The biggest difference between happy and unhappy people in general isn't the number or severity of their problems. It's their skill at solving them. Happy people (1) have more effective problem-solving strategies, and (2) *believe* in their ability to make positive changes in their lives. More about the second part later. Right now, let's examine some of the key problem-solving strategies used by unhappy people.

Problem-Solving Strategies Guaranteed to Fail

1. **Short-term rather than long-term solutions.** When problems persist, it may be that you are focusing on short-term answers. You're trying to feel better, in the moment, rather than planning long-term solutions that are hard now, but will eventually create enduring change. The classic example is giving in versus setting limits for a misbehaving child. When you give in to kids' unreasonable demands, the child's gratitude and the sudden drop in noise level are very rewarding. In the moment. But down the line, there will be a lot more tears and tantrums. The long-term solution is to set limits and endure the unpleasantness while a tantrum burns itself out. It isn't fun, but eventually you'll deal with a lot less problem behavior.

2. **Numbing.** This solution focuses on blocking the pain. Alcohol, drugs, TV and computer addictions, escapist socializing, compulsive risk-taking, and compulsive sexual behavior are just a few of the numbing strategies. While numbing helps you temporarily escape your feelings about a problem, nothing gets solved. In fact, the problem is usually getting worse the whole time you're running away.

3. **Trying to change others.** The fallacy here is that people change. But they don't, not because you want them to, anyway. So you get angry. You complain and you blame. But nothing happens. And the more you try to push or coerce others to solve your problems, the more helpless you become. Consider the example of a man who feels lonely and empty. He tries to fix it by demanding that his wife be more attentive, more sexual. Nothing changes, so he cranks up the volume on his complaints. Sadly, his wife seems to withdraw more, which only deepens his feelings of loneliness.

4. **Waiting.** This future-oriented strategy assumes things will get better—after the kids leave home, after you retire, after your boss retires, after your promotion, after your Uncle Otto kicks and leaves you something in his will. The unfortunate thing about waiting is that you do nothing to resolve problems in the present. You feel more hopeful perhaps, expecting time to fix things, but there's no guarantee. And meanwhile, life is less than satisfying.

5. **Setting phony prerequisites and irrelevant goals.** Before you take a career-advancing real estate course, you feel compelled to buy a new desk, get your house appraised, and put stepping stones in the garden. None of the phony prerequisites are relevant or necessary. They just sabotage or delay your plans.

6. **Setting phony prerequisites and impossible goals.** Before you can start dating and socializing, you feel compelled to lose forty pounds—which proves too hard to do. Before you can start writing the novel you've always dreamed about, you feel compelled to finish your B.A. in English—which you lack the time, money, and motivation to complete.

7. **Over-reaching.** Your plan to solve the problem is so complex, and requires so much energy, that you collapse before ever really starting. The plan is based on an ideal, an impossible standard that some part of you knows you can never reach. In fact, subconsciously, that's why you're over-reaching and expecting so much of yourself. This way you'll stay stuck and you won't have to face change.

8. **Going under, so you can be rescued.** This problem-solving strategy requires that you let things get really bad. Unconsciously, the plan is to appear as if you're drowning emotionally—overwhelmed, going down. Then someone who cares will hopefully step in and take action. Trouble is sometimes they don't. Or they try, but don't know how to help. Or it's just too late.

We're putting the strategies that don't work right upfront because knowing what *not* to do is crucial. If you sometimes use any of the above eight problem-solving techniques, start right now being on guard. The more you can avoid these classic dead-ends, the better your chances become to make real changes in your life.

Problem Solving That Works

The problem-solving method you'll learn here is based on a five-step strategy pioneered by Thomas D'Zurilla and Marvin Goldfried (1971). They define a problem as "failure to find an effective response," and their approach spurs both creative thinking and careful evaluation of alternative solutions. Clinical studies have shown D'Zurilla and Goldfried's method works. Thousands of people have used it effectively. And if you follow each step, it will bring positive change to your life as well.

We've updated and modernized the technique. It's now called A to E Problem Solving. This core method has been proven effective over the course of thirty years and across an incredible variety of problems.

When Do You Need Problem Solving?

You can tell it's time for serious problem solving when you face one of the following three conditions:

1. A situation in your life triggers a persistent and painful emotion. Even though time goes by, you continue to feel angry, sad, anxious, lonely, ashamed, guilty, or overwhelmed.

2. You find yourself in conflict with significant people in your life. And you feel stuck because each person has very different needs in the situation.

3. You want something very much, yet face roadblocks that threaten to keep you feeling helpless and stuck.

If any of these conditions are present in your life—now or in the future—you should commence steps A to E of this problem-solving program.

Blocks to Problem Solving—Core Beliefs

There's one "problem" with problem solving. Some people can't seem to work through the simple steps—something gets in the way. What blocks them is a negative schema, or core belief, about who they are and what they're capable of.

Your core beliefs are really a kind of self-portrait. They set your sights and establish your basic fears. They are the basis of most major life decisions. When your self-portrait is full of flaws and blemishes, it warns you that you won't be appreciated and well received. It warns you to expect pain and loss and failure in life.

The core beliefs that make up your self-portrait were formed early in life. They grew from thousands of interactions and experiences in your family of origin. Most of them you probably don't remember. But they all become part of who you think you are and what you expect from life. They are, very simply, your identity.

The following four core beliefs are most often implicated in keeping you stuck and helpless. They affect your ability to problem solve because they (1) make you believe it won't work, or (2) make you believe you don't deserve to have your needs met. These core beliefs are:

- **I'm incompetent.** This is the conviction that you can't do things right. You expect to fail, screw up, or blow it. Every time you consider an alternative solution, the thought comes up, "I couldn't do that." And with it, a feeling of anxiety that you'll be humiliated if you try. Everyone will see you fall on your face. Your best strategy is to avoid trying. Because if you don't try, you don't screw up. Problem solving becomes very difficult because overwhelming anxiety can stop you from taking even the first steps to implement your new plan.

- **I'm unworthy.** This is the conviction, and feeling, that you are flawed, bad, wrong, and undeserving. When you are influenced by this core belief, it's scary to push for your needs. You expect people to be annoyed and to reject you if you ask for something or try to change things. You assume that you, and your problem, don't have much importance. And your best strategy is to endure and hope things will somehow get better. When attempting to problem solve, people with this core belief often have trouble putting their needs into words. They can't imagine any solution that others would support or help with.

- **I'm not safe.** This is the assumption that the world is a dangerous and uncertain place. You can't rely on anything, and must always remain vigilant. Change of any kind is especially dangerous because you can't always predict what will happen. Your conviction is that if something bad *could* happen, it probably *will* happen. And your best strategy is to avoid change of any kind, particularly something that might catapult you out of your stuck but predictable place. When attempting problem solving, people with the core belief that they aren't safe often assess each alternative solution to be too dangerous. They turn even the slightest uncertainty about an outcome into likely catastrophe.

- **Others' needs have primacy.** This belief requires that the needs of others should always come first. Psychologist Jeffrey Young (1999) calls this core belief "subjugation," because in any conflict the impulse is to give in and defer to other people. While sometimes associated with unworthiness, this core belief has a vector of its own. It's not so much that you are unimportant, it's just that others' needs are more important. You empathize with them. You understand their pain, their desires. And it eclipses any sense of your own. When you endorse this core belief, problem solving is difficult because you can't seek solutions that would conflict *in any way* with the needs of people you care about.

Before starting actual problem solving, it's important to determine if any of these four core beliefs might be sabotaging your efforts. In the next section, you'll find an inventory that will help you assess the strength of these key beliefs. It will give you a sense of how much they might be influencing, or limiting, your current problem-solving efforts.

After each of the forty statements that follow, circle T or F according to whether you think the statement is mostly true or mostly false. In cases where it's a close decision, go with your first impulse. It's important to complete every item, circling the T or the F (but not both), in order to get an accurate score at the end. Remember, this is not a test—there are no right or wrong answers, or better or worse ways to complete the inventory.

Assessing Your Core Beliefs
Core Belief Inventory

(Adapted from McKay and Fanning [1991])

	Mostly True	Mostly False	
1a.*	T	F	I am worthy of love and respect.
2b.*	T	F	My world is a pretty safe place.
3c.*	T	F	I perform many tasks well.
4d.*	T	F	I try to take care of the things I need, even if it sometimes disappoints someone else.
5a.	T	F	I often feel flawed or defective.
6b.	T	F	Life is dangerous—a medical, natural, or financial disaster could strike at any time.
7c.	T	F	I'm basically incompetent.
8d.	T	F	I sometimes tend to sacrifice my own needs in order to take care of others.
9a.*	T	F	I feel okay about myself.
10b.*	T	F	I can protect myself from most dangers.
11c.*	T	F	Doing some things comes easy to me.
12d.*	T	F	It's very important to know what you want and to try to go after it, even if others don't agree.
13a.	T	F	Nobody I desire would desire me if they really got to know me.
14b.	T	F	I worry about getting sick or hurt.
15c.	T	F	When I trust my own judgment, I make wrong decisions.
16d.	T	F	I rarely think about myself, or what I need, because I'm so aware of what others' feel.
17a.*	T	F	I have legitimate needs that I deserve to fill.
18b.*	T	F	I am willing to take risks.

19c.*	T	F	I am a competent person, as capable as most people.
20d.*	T	F	People have to take care of themselves, first and foremost.
21a.	T	F	I am dull and boring and can't make interesting conversation.
22b.	T	F	If I'm not careful with myself, I might end up with nothing.
23c.	T	F	I tend to avoid new challenges.
24d.	T	F	One of my rules in life is to try to avoid conflict.
25a.*	T	F	I count for something in the world.
26b.*	T	F	I can take care of myself and my loved ones.
27c.*	T	F	I can learn new skills if I try.
28d.*	T	F	I'll fight for what I want in life, even if people try to stand in my way.
29a.	T	F	I'm unattractive.
30b.	T	F	I choose my old, familiar ways of doing things over risking the unexpected.
31c.	T	F	I don't perform well under stress.
32d.	T	F	A family is a place where people take care of each other more than themselves.
33a.*	T	F	People I like and respect often like and respect me.
34b.*	T	F	I don't worry much about health or money.
35c.*	T	F	Almost all of my decisions are sound.
36d.*	T	F	When my needs conflict with someone else's, I usually try to explain my need and why it's important to me.
37a.	T	F	I don't deserve much attention or respect.
38b.	T	F	I feel uneasy when I go very far from home alone.
39c.	T	F	I mess up everything I attempt.
40d.	T	F	I tend to defer to others about choice of restaurant or entertainment. I'd rather keep the peace than push for my preference.

Scoring

This inventory assesses our core beliefs about the four topics listed below. High scores for any of these core beliefs may indicate an important psychological block to effective problem solving. To score your answers, follow these instructions carefully.

1. **Competence** _____ points

   Look at your "c" answers (3c, 7c, 11c, and so on). For any "c" answer with an asterisk (*) that you marked FALSE, give yourself one point. For any "c" answer without an asterisk that you marked TRUE, give yourself one point. Record your total points in the space above.

   On a scale of one to ten, this indicates how much you *disagree* with the statement "I am competent." The higher your score, the less competent you feel.

2. **Self-Worth** _____ points

   Look at your "a" answers (1a, 5a, 9a, and so on). For any "a" answer with an asterisk (*) that you marked FALSE, give yourself one point. For any "a" answer without an asterisk that you marked TRUE, give yourself one point. Record your total points in the space above.

   On a scale of one to ten, this indicates how much you *disagree* with the statement "I am worthy." The higher your score, the less you may tend to value yourself as a person.

3. **Safety** _____ points

   Look at your "b" answers (2b, 6b, 10b, and so on). For any "b" answer with an asterisk (*) that you marked FALSE, give yourself one point. For any "b" answer without an asterisk that you marked TRUE, give yourself one point. Record your total points in the space above.

   On a scale of one to ten, this indicates how much you *disagree* with the statement "I am safe." The higher your score, the less safe (and perhaps more anxious) you feel.

4. **Primacy of Your Needs** _____ points

   Look at your "d" answers (4d, 8d, 12d, and so on). For any "d" answer with an asterisk (*) that you marked FALSE, give yourself one point. For any "d" answer without an asterisk that you marked TRUE, give yourself one point. Record your total points in the space above.

   On a scale of one to ten, this indicates how much you *disagree* with the statement "my needs are as important as others'." The higher your score, the more you tend to defer to others' needs.

Interpreting the Results

The core beliefs inventory is just a guideline. It's designed to help you recognize the influence of key beliefs, not to pass judgment on them or yourself. Scores should be seen as indications that a particular core belief may be affecting you whenever you attempt to change your life. Scores above 5 suggest that the belief plays at least some role in your decisions. The closer the score is to 10, the more rigid and limiting the belief is likely to be.

What to Do

If you scored between 6 and 10 on any of the core beliefs, we recommend that you go immediately to the chapter covering that belief, before continuing with the problem-solving steps. Commit to really working on the exercises and experiments in that chapter. This can only increase your chances of success. If you didn't score above 5 for any of the beliefs, or are convinced that they don't influence your problem-solving efforts, skip to Chapter 7 on Assessment. That's the first official step in your problem-solving program.

2

The Core Belief of Competence

The belief that you aren't competent to solve a problem can defeat you before you start. This chapter is about (1) learning how this belief works to paralyze you, and (2) challenging the belief so you can get free to make changes in your life. The first step is to map the structure and impact of your core belief.

Mapping Your Core Belief

In a few pages you'll find a blank Core Belief Worksheet to help you explore beliefs regarding competence. The first question on the worksheet is, "What's your belief?" Write in your own words what you believe about your competence to solve problems in general. What do you think will happen if you attempt to try something new, learn a different strategy, make an attempt to "fix" things? Right now, in that section of your worksheet, put a description of what you *think* will happen if you try new problem-solving solutions.

A psychotherapist who was trying to solve anger problems in his marriage wrote this: "I'll make a plan and screw it up. I won't remember what I'm supposed to do; I won't do it right. Things will end up worse than when I started."

The second question on the worksheet is, "What feelings does it bring?" Write down your emotional reaction when something happens to make you question your competence. Do you feel scared, sad, ashamed, guilty, angry?

A school teacher who was trying to solve classroom behavior problems wrote this: "Every lame attempt to solve the problem gets me scared and depressed; I feel like a failure."

The third question on the worksheet is, "Where does it come from?" Here you should write about early messages from parents and other family members about your competence. Significant or embarrassing early failures might also be worth noting here.

A salesman, who wanted to improve his performance, noted in this section that his father would get angry after giving him a painting or home repair project. "He never had a good word to say about anything I did; I never did it right."

The fourth question is, "What are the triggers?" Under this question are a list of eight key arenas for you to explore. Ask yourself these following questions. What emotions trigger my core belief that I'm not competent? What events in my relationships trigger thoughts and feelings of incompetence; what career or work issues trigger a sense of incompetence, and so on? Try to fill in as much as you can think of for each arena. Use a separate page if you need it.

The fifth question on the worksheet is, "What are your compensating behaviors?" This is an opportunity to explore what you do when you start feeling incompetent. How do you cope when something in a relationship triggers these feelings? How do you cope when you get scared that you'll screw up? How do you cope when you need to fix or change something and it seems beyond your abilities? Compensating behaviors for feelings of incompetence often involve avoidance, getting people to do a task for you, waiting too long and then doing a half-baked job, and so on.

Example

This Core Belief Worksheet was filled out by Jerry, a nurse who wanted to do a better job supervising his son's homework. Core beliefs about competence made it hard to push the boy and assist him to do higher quality school work.

Jerry's Core Belief Worksheet

What's your belief (in your own words)?

I won't do it right. Whatever I do won't work.

What feelings does it bring?

Anxiety, feelings of embarrassment, a kind of despair that I could never change anything.

Where does it come from (in your family of origin)?

My father told me I was an idiot. Always having my brothers fix things I screwed up. The static electricity machine I built for science project that gave Dad a bad electric shock. My mother telling me not to become a nurse because their mistakes kill people.

What are the triggers?

Emotions: *When I'm anxious.*

Relationships: *When someone counts on me or expects something of me. When someone's judging my performance.*

Work/Career: *When I've been given a patient with a new treatment protocol, a new machine to learn, or the charge nurse is irritated about something.*

Education/Knowledge: *Chemotherapy protocols—I feel like I don't know enough about the dangers and potential problems. Don't know enough math or chemistry to help my son at school.*

Money: *Won't make the right decision regarding retirement and investments.*

Recreation/Pleasure: *I'm not sure I really understand what turns my wife on, how to satisfy her sexually.*

Environment: *I'm nervous when I'm supposed to fix something around the house. Always worried I won't do it right.*

Health: N/A

What are your compensating behaviors for:

Emotional triggers? *Avoid things when I'm scared.*

Relationship triggers? *I put things off, tell people I'm going to fail. I try to be perfect and then screw it up.*

Work/Career triggers? *Keep getting people to do things for me, constantly ask questions, make self-depreciating jokes.*

Education/Knowledge triggers? *Try to avoid, get people to help, get my wife to supervise John's homework.*

Money triggers? *Put off decision, be totally conservative. Get friends to advise me.*

Recreation/Pleasure triggers? *Do things the same old way/don't say anything. Don't ask wife what she feels.*

Environment triggers? *Put it off. Hire people to fix things around the house without investigating their qualifications.*

Health triggers? N/A

It's Your Turn

On the next page is a blank copy of the worksheet you've been learning how to fill out. If you're not sure what to do in a particular section, go back to the example worksheet and try to use that as a model. Remember, this is an opportunity to get at the root of what's keeping you stuck, so it's important to be honest with your answers.

My Core Belief Worksheet

What's your belief (in your own words)?

What feelings does it bring?

Where does it come from (in your family of origin)?

What are the triggers?

Emotions:

Relationships:

Work/Career:

Education/Knowledge:

Money:

Recreation/Pleasure:

Environment:

Health:

What are your compensating behaviors for:

Emotional triggers?

Relationship triggers?

Work/Career triggers?

Education/Knowledge triggers?

Money triggers?

Recreation/Pleasure triggers?

Environment triggers?

Health triggers?

How Your Core Belief Influences Problem Solving

Now it's time to get specific. We need to explore precisely how your core belief regarding competence is getting in the way of what you want to change. You bought this book for a reason. Something isn't right; things in your life need to change. The first step is to identify the problems you want to solve.

In the left-hand column of the worksheet that follows, write down at least three problems you've struggled (but failed) to solve in the past few years.

You've gotten familiar with compensating behaviors from the Core Beliefs Worksheet you just completed. Now you have a chance to examine which of them may have sabotaged your problem-solving efforts. Did you find yourself avoiding when you needed to work at your new solution? Did you try, and then give up? Did you try to get someone else to do it? Did you set too high a goal, and then become overwhelmed? Whatever compensating behaviors you may have used, describe them in the right-hand column of the worksheet below. Remember that compensating behaviors are a way to cope with your core belief about competence. If you need help identifying them, return to the filled-in example of the Core Belief Worksheet and check out the section on compensating behaviors you'll find there.

Example

Here's Henry's filled out Problem-Solving Worksheet to give you an idea of how to do this exercise. Notice that the column headed "Problems You've Attempted to Solve" includes both a description of the problem as well as an attempted solution.

Henry's Problem-Solving Worksheet

Problems You've Attempted to Solve	Compensating Behaviors
1. Try to solve my financial problems by making a budget.	1. Put off working on it. 2. Couldn't seem to find information about quarterlies and key expenses. 3. Tried to get Lucy to do it. 4. Set times to work on it and forgot.
2. Children might overhear love-making—agree to put up sound board on wall.	1. Put off calling contractor. 2. Complained and blamed partner for being concerned about the problem.
3. Mother is very critical of wife—agree to talk to her before summer visit.	1. Put it off. 2. Tell mother we're very busy, and no good time to visit this summer. 3. Get angry and tell wife she should deal with problem herself.

My Problem-Solving Worksheet

Problems You've Attempted to Solve	Compensating Behaviors
1.	1. 2. 3.
2.	1. 2. 3.
3.	1. 2. 3.
4.	1. 2. 3.
5.	1. 2. 3.
6.	1. 2. 3.

Using What You've Learned

The belief that you aren't competent, and the accompanying fear of failure, triggers compensating behaviors. These behaviors end up reinforcing and strengthening the belief that you'll fail. It's like a self-fulfilling prophecy. When you fear failure, you avoid challenges or do a half-baked job. And then you really do end up failing. Not because you're incompetent, but because you ran away from the challenge. From now on, you need to monitor all your problem-solving efforts—watching for the first sign of your old compensating behaviors. Then stop them. Immediately. And replace them with the coping plan you'll develop later in this chapter. The key is vigilance. Don't let the compensating behaviors really get started.

Testing Your Core Belief

How True Is Your Core Belief?

Core beliefs, by their nature, are generalities. They reflect what is sometimes, but not always, true. One way to test your core belief about competence is to explore exceptions to the rule. When did you do something really well? What moments in your life are marked by the satisfaction that you accomplished something you set out to do? In the space provided below, list every single experience you can think of where you were satisfied with your performance. Also include any situation where others praised you for something you did well. To do this exercise correctly, you'll need to carefully review your life from childhood on. Write down anything you remember that suggests competence—whether it was getting a good grade in a difficult course or successfully planting a new lawn. It doesn't matter how big or little the item is in the scope of a lifetime, just put it down.

Here is an Exceptions to the Rule Worksheet filled out by Todd, a twenty-four-year old graphic artist.

Todd's Exceptions to the Rule Worksheet

Age	Situation	What I Did
4	Preschool play—scared	Nervous in the beginning—everyone liked it.
7	Cub Scout badge	Got discouraged, but made myself work a whole weekend putting wildflower project together.
9	"Black holes" presentation	Nervous, but I warmed up and did well.
13	Chairman—dance committee	Pulled together a lot of loose ends and put on a great 8th grade dance.
15	Sophomore Spanish	Totally freaked because I couldn't remember vocabulary. But got B+.
16	Attracted to Cathy	Kept sitting with her at lunch till she went out with me.
17	Baseball team	Kept practicing in the batting cage till I was good enough to make the team.
18	College	Got into UC Santa Cruz—1st choice.
19	Photography Exhibit	"Railroad Crossing" took 2nd place.
20	Photography Exhibit	Did 17 photograph shows—3 straight days in the dark room.
21	Wanted to be with Cathy	Engineered transfer to UCLA to be with her.
21	Mom's accident	Got her a better physical therapist and made her do the exercises—a success!
22	UCLA Exhibit	I was scared, but selected, finished, and mounted 29 photographs in 3 weeks.
23	Job hunting	Kept at it till I aced interview at CaliGraphics.
23	Cathy hates our apartment	After a month of heavy searching, found a great place in the Oakland hills.

My Exceptions to the Rule Worksheet

Age	Situation	What I Did

Looking at the Whole Picture

To get a clearer picture of how competently you function in the world it's necessary to systematically evaluate each area of your life. What follows is the Self-Concept Inventory (adapted from McKay and Fanning 2001), an exercise for exploring how you function in each of the following eight domains:

1. *Relating to family.* One-sentence descriptions of your strengths and weaknesses in your relationships to family members.

2. *Relating to friends.* One-sentence descriptions of your strengths and weaknesses in your relationships to your friends.

3. *Relating to people you don't know.* One-sentence descriptions of your strengths and weaknesses as you relate to people you don't know.

4. *How others see you.* One-sentence descriptions of the strengths and weaknesses that your friends and family see.

5. *Performance at school or on the job.* One-sentence descriptions of the way you handle the major tasks at school or work.

6. *Performance of the daily tasks of life.* Descriptions could include such areas as hygiene, health, maintenance of your living environment, food preparation, caring for your children, and any other ways you take care of personal or family needs.

7. *Mental functioning.* Include one-sentence assessments of how well you reason and solve problems, your capacity for learning and creativity, your general fund of knowledge, your areas of special knowledge, wisdom you've acquired, insight, and so on.

8. *Sexuality.* One-sentence descriptions of how you see and feel about yourself as a sexual person.

In a moment you'll take the Self-Concept Inventory. When you do, be honest. Try to think of positives as well as negatives. Because you may be inclined to remember more negative than positive experiences, you'll need to compensate for this tendency by really mining your memory for positive nuggets. When you are finished with the inventory, go back and put a plus (+) by items that represent strengths or things you like about yourself. Put a minus (−) by items that you consider weaknesses or would like to change about yourself.

It's going to take a little work to list as many brief descriptions as you can think of in each of these eight domains. But the result will be to achieve a broader, more accurate picture of your abilities.

Self-Concept Inventory

1. Relating to Family

_____

_____

2. Relating to Friends

_____

_____

3. Relating to People You Don't Know

_____

_____

4. How Others See You

_____

_____

5. Performance at School or on the Job

_____

_____

6. Performance of the Daily Tasks of Life

_____

_____

7. Mental Functioning

_____

_____

8. Sexuality

_____

_____

Now take a fresh look at the weaknesses—the things you marked with a minus. Using the Re-Evaluation Worksheet that follows, you're going to rewrite these descriptions to make them a little more accurate. There are four rules you need to follow when you begin revising the items on your list of weaknesses.

1. *Use non-pejorative language.* For example, "Shop stupidly" should be rewritten as, "Too many trips to the grocery store because I buy just what I need for dinner

that night." "Fatally passive" should be rewritten as, "Avoid conflict when people seem to be getting angry." Make sure you eliminate all words that have a negative connotation—stupid, blabber mouth, wishy washy, lousy, bumbling, and so on. These words are attacks, not descriptions.

2. Use accurate language. Don't exaggerate and don't embellish the negative. Revise the items on your weaknesses list so that they are purely descriptive. Confine yourself to the facts. For example, "Never ask for what I want" would probably need to be rewritten as, "Ask for what I want only when very comfortable and safe with a person." "Screw up paperwork" is probably inaccurate because it over-generalizes. You'd need to identify what, specifically, you forget or mishandle on the paperwork.

3. *Use language that is specific rather than general.* Eliminate words like everything, always, never, completely, and so on. Rewrite your list so that your descriptions are limited to the particular situation, setting, or relationship. General indictments, such as "Can't set limits or say no," should be revised to reflect only the specific relationships where the problem occurs. "Get angry all the time" is another example of being too general. You need to identify who makes you angry, as well as the situations.

4. *Find exceptions or corresponding strengths.* This is an essential step for those items that really make you feel bad about your abilities. For everything you list that you do wrong, there's probably a time you did it right. For every weakness, there's some kind of balancing strength that compensates. An item such as "Mentally lazy" might be rewritten as, "Bored by political and philosophical issues, abstract thought. Do like to think about motivations and drives behind human behavior." Notice that the revision makes the weakness more specific, but also emphasizes a balancing strength.

To complete the Re-Evaluation Worksheet, just write down each negative description in the left-hand column. In the right-hand column, rewrite your description following the four principles discussed above.

The following is a Re-Evaluation Worksheet filled out by a forty-five-year-old school teacher.

Gary's Re-Evaluation Worksheet

Negative Description	Revised Description
1. Shy	Cautious with strangers; outgoing with friends.
2. Judgmental	Strong opinions about how people should treat each other.
3. Uncomfortable and awkward	I have a formality, but I also treat people with respect.
4. Big conflict avoider	Look for common ground and points of agreement.
5. Tired all the time	Good energy in the morning; run out of gas by 7-8 P.M.
6. Easily confused	Don't multitask well; but can stay effective and focused for single task.
7. Poor general appearance	Don't care about clothes or fashion; stay neat and clean.
8. Can't cook	Only cook simple things; put energy into writing fiction.
9. A know-nothing on current events	But I know 19th-century history.
10. Boring conversationalist	With strangers I'm shut down; but I can be animated with friends.
11. Uncreative	I teach with a pretty strict formula—but I write creatively.
12. Very sexually controlled	It takes a long time for me to build trust, but I let go more as I do.

My Re-Evaluation Worksheet

Negative Description	Revised Description

Putting It All Together

What have you learned so far? After reviewing your Exceptions to the Rule Worksheet, your Self-Concept Inventory, and your Re-Evaluation Worksheet, is there anything new in how you think about your competence? Is your core belief softening, changing, or in any way different after doing these exercises? Go back to your Core Belief Worksheet now, and read the words you used to describe your beliefs about competence. In the space below rewrite that statement, incorporating some of the exceptions and strengths you've just worked to discover.

What's Your Belief—Revised

3

The Core Belief of Worth

If you believe deep down that you are worthless, every problem becomes insurmountable. This chapter will teach you how doubting your own worth keeps you from solving problems, and how overcoming that doubt can make it easier to solve all kinds of problems. The first step is to map the structure and impact of your core belief.

Mapping Your Core Belief

In a few pages you'll find a blank Core Belief Worksheet. It will help you explore your belief about self-worth. The first question of the worksheet is, "What's your belief?" In this space, write down the essence of your belief in your own words. Put it in terms of what you think will happen if you seriously attempted to solve a major problem in your life. Go ahead and fill out the first question now, predicting what you think might happen if you attempt to solve your problem.

A technical assistant who worked for the county Roads & Bridges Department was thinking about applying for a promotion to the civil engineer's office. When she contemplated trying to make this happen, she wrote, "They'd never pick someone like me anyway, and I'd be totally humiliated to try something and be passed over."

The next question on the worksheet is, "What feelings does it bring?" Here you should write down the feelings you have when some event or person questions your worth. Do you feel ashamed, embarrassed, shy, afraid, nervous, guilty, flustered, or frightened?

A cancer patient who was dreading a confrontation with her oncologist wrote, "I feel stupid and small, ashamed to draw attention to myself, a sickly, whining creature that I myself wouldn't pay much attention to."

The third question on the worksheet, "Where does it come from?" refers to the source of the feeling in your earliest experiences growing up in your family of origin. When you relive this feeling as a youngster, what is going on? Who is sending you messages of worthlessness? What was said or done or not done that made you feel insignificant?

A daycare worker remembered times in her family when all the attention was on her rebellious older sister and her attention deficit younger brother. Whenever she wanted some attention she was told to shut up and stop making things worse. She wrote: "Everybody and everything skipped over the middle child like I wasn't there."

The fourth question is, "What are the triggers?" For each of the key problem areas listed under the question, try to come up with one feeling, situation, experience, or event that triggers your feelings of worthlessness and shame. Take your time and be as thorough and detailed as possible, using extra paper if you need the room.

The fifth question on the worksheet is, "What are your compensating behaviors?" and the spaces for reply are divided into the same categories as the previous question. For each problem area, describe *what you do* when feelings of worthlessness arise. When you feel one-down and undeserving in a close relationship, what do you do to compensate? Clam up? Start a fight? Bury yourself in a book or TV? When shameful feelings are triggered about the quality or scope of your education, what do you do to compensate? Boast about your street smarts? Belittle others' knowledge? Change the subject to something you're the expert on? Compensating behavior can take the form of avoidance, counter attack, procrastination, passing the buck, and so on.

Example

This Core Belief Worksheet was completed by Stella, a part-time model, actress, and product demonstrator who, at forty-two years old, was seeing more and more paying gigs going to younger women. She had vague aspirations to move into sales with one of the local businesses for whom she demonstrated products at trade shows, but she couldn't seem to get moving.

Stella's Core Belief Worksheet

What's your belief (in your own words)?

I'm of very little use to anyone.

If I applied to the other company, they'd see right through me, and laugh in my face for putting myself forward.

What feelings does it bring?

Embarrassed.

Ashamed of being a has-been.

Depressed by getting older, uglier.

Envious of younger women in acting.

Resentful of successful women my age.

Where does it come from (in your family of origin)?

Mom said I'd never amount to more than a pretty face.

Dad ignored me till puberty, paid too much attention after that.

Brother Dave tossed my book report in the garbage, said, "Stick to baton twirling."

What are the triggers?

Emotions—Lately when I get excited about an audition, I feel a creepy sort of dread that is different from the giddy stage fright I used to feel.

Relationships—When someone starts ignoring me, assuming he can make decisions for me and I'm too wimpy to speak up.

Work/Career—Whenever I audition, apply for a demo job. Especially when I think about asking for a regular salaried position. When I try to make fifteen years of smiling and pointing to water softeners and Xerox machines sound like real sales experience.

Education/Knowledge—When I imagine filling out a real job application, and I realize that those years of acting and voice workshops add up to exactly zippo in the real job world—they're a dead giveaway that I'm a wornout piece of fluff.

Money—Health benefits? Savings? Retirement? Hah! That's what grown-ups have, not overgrown cheerleaders like me.

Recreation/Pleasure—In the middle of a party, and I still do love to party, God help me—I'll think, "We're all going to die, what's the use?"

Environment—When I look at the crappy studio apartment that twenty years of showbiz has earned me, I feel like the chump of all time.

Health—Whenever a new ache or bump shows up and I think, "Can I afford to have this looked into?"

What are your compensating behaviors for:

Emotional triggers?—Criticize myself in advance before an audition by thinking: "Don't get your hopes up, grandma, you're too old for the part."

Relationship triggers?—I dump them before they can dump me.

Work/Career triggers?—I downplay my need and seriousness, try to give the impression I'm in it for the laughs, don't care what happens.

Education/Knowledge triggers?—*I put on this bouncy Judy Garland "I can do anything" air that sounds faker and faker as I age.*

Money triggers?—*I buy a new scarf and a bottle of champagne.*

Recreation/Pleasure triggers?—*I stay too late, party too hard to prove to myself that I'm still twenty-one years old.*

Environment triggers?—*Put off looking for a better place, asking for improvements. Let the super walk all over me.*

Health triggers?—*Joke about "Stay gorgeous, die young."*

It's Your Turn

On the next page is a blank copy of the worksheet you've been learning about. If you get to a particular section and can't remember how to fill it out, go back to the relevant instructions above. Remember this is an opportunity to get at the root of what's keeping you stuck, so it's important to be honest with your answers.

My Core Belief Worksheet

What's your belief (in your own words)?

What feelings does it bring?

Where does it come from (in your family of origin)?

What are the triggers?

Emotions

Relationships

Work/Career

Education/Knowledge

Money

Recreation/Pleasure

Environment

Health

What are your compensating behaviors for:

Emotional triggers?

Relationship triggers?

Work/Career triggers?

Education/Knowledge triggers?

Money triggers?

Recreation/Pleasure triggers?

Environment triggers?

Health triggers?

How Your Core Belief Influences Problem Solving

In this section you will explore how your core belief gets in the way of making important changes in your life. To get started, identify some problems in your life that you would like to solve, but have not had any success with in recent years. In the first column of the worksheet that follows, write down at least three things you have been struggling to accomplish. If you have trouble thinking up problems, ask yourself what went through your mind when you decided to buy and read this book.

When you have at least three problems written down on the left, move on to the right-hand column. Here you will list compensating behaviors—things you have done in response to the problem that didn't actually solve it. What have you done to sabotage your problem-solving efforts? Did you procrastinate? Distract yourself with something else? Deny, rationalize, or minimize the problem? Lash out at someone? Try to get someone else to solve it? Avoid working on the problem? Create a new problem? Give up?

These are the same types of items you wrote down in the last part of the preceding worksheet. Return to that list if you have trouble remembering your typical compensating behaviors. Remember that compensating behaviors are ways to cope with your core belief about your own worthlessness, lack of value, or undeserving nature. What did you do to assuage, drown out, or deny the feelings aroused by this belief?

Example

Here is a Problem-Solving Worksheet filled out Steve, by a computer security expert who has a teenage daughter, a pre-ulcerous colon, and a wife who might be in love with another woman.

My Problem-Solving Worksheet	
Problems You've Attempted to Solve	**Compensating Behaviors**
1. Talk to daughter Karen about smell of pot in her room	1. Put it off. 2. Try to get wife to deal with it. 3. Planned to bring it up while driving to movies, then chickened out. 4. Hassle her about grades and phone calls instead.
2. Make appointment with stomach doctor, get Tagamet, or ?	1. Lost doctor's phone number twice. 2. Make an appointment and cancel at last minute. 3. Blame health plan for delays & obstructions. 4. Try dumb home remedies like warm milk and honey.
3. Confront wife Mel about all the time spent with her lesbian creative writing instructor.	1. Refuse to think about it—don't be silly. 2. Find myself "forgetting" it's class night and planning a dinner out or going to a play. 3. Give up. Tell myself, "I've lost her, she has nothing but contempt for me." 4. Start big fights over anything: Karen's allowance, how she drives, the meaning of the word *idiosyncratic*. 5. Panic in the middle of a fight and start apologizing, groveling.

My Problem-Solving Worksheet

Problems You've Attempted to Solve	Compensating Behaviors
1.	1. 2. 3.
2.	1. 2. 3.
3.	1. 2. 3.
4.	1. 2. 3.
5.	1. 2. 3.

Using What You've Learned

Hopefully you're starting to see the static pattern caused by low self-esteem. The belief that you are unworthy or valueless triggers compensating behaviors like giving up or avoidance, which in turn reinforce the belief that you're not worth much. When you fear exposure of your worthlessness, when you avoid any public scrutiny of your value, you stop trying very hard, you stop putting yourself out there very far. You circumscribe your world with a very small list of things that can be done by such a small person. It becomes a self-fulfilling prophecy that little people do very little, and that just proves how little they really are.

The way out of this closed cycle of low self-esteem and low efficacy is to begin monitoring all your problem-solving attempts. Whenever you notice that you are slipping into one of your typical compensating behaviors, you need to tell yourself, "Stop." Then you will replace the compensating behavior with one of the new coping behaviors that you will develop later in this chapter. The key is to stay alert and stop compensating behaviors before they get started.

Testing Your Core Belief

By their very nature, core beliefs are generalities. They are based on what is sometimes, but not always, true. You can test your core beliefs about worth by looking at exceptions to the rule. Identify times in your past when you lived up to your values, did the right thing, accomplished something you felt good about, overcame a hardship, displayed courage and self-reliance, or were generous, supportive, or loving to others. In the form below, write down everything you can remember that runs counter to the notion that you lack value or worth—every time you displayed integrity, intelligence, compassion, love, or other positive qualities. It doesn't matter how minor these exceptions now seem or how long ago they occurred. Just write down as many as you can.

Example

Here is an Exceptions to the Rule Worksheet filled out by Geena, a twenty-nine-year-old hair stylist, poet, and astrologer in New Jersey who wanted to move to Oregon.

Geena's Exceptions to the Rule Worksheet

Age	Situation	What I Did
5	Kindergarten	Was new kid Mary Lou's play pal and helped her fit in.
7	Birthday party	Invited two kids who were ostracized.
10	Neighbor's pet	Took good care of Mrs. Gryzski's poodle.
14	Police station	Turned in the money Gracie and I found.
14	Poetry	First sonnet got into junior high yearbook.
16–18	Divorce	Walked a tightrope between mom and dad, peacemaker.
19	Write up in school paper	"Poetess of the Stars" astrology t-shirt.
20	Bill	Took notes for him when he broke his leg.
21	Bill's drinking and late hours	Refrained from ratting him out to parole officer after he dumped me.
21	First job	Did well at Marlene's Mane Event until the fire.
22	Prom season	Washed, streaked, cut, and styled thirteen teenyboppers in two days.
24–26	Astrological charts	Though I was super busy, cast real charts instead of faking them.
26	Heather's breakup	Hid her out and helped her move three times in one year.
27	Mom's breakdown	Dropped everything to help her.
28	Art Center Literary Fair	Read two of my poems despite stage fright.

My Exceptions to the Rule Worksheet

Age	Situation	What I Did

What Others See

In this exercise you will recall much of the positive feedback you have received from others. In the form below, enter your age, the other person's name, the situation, and the positive feedback you received. Try to remember all the family members, friends, strangers, romantic partners, teachers, counselors, religious figures, bosses, co-workers, and so on who have made positive remarks to you or shown their approval in any other way.

Example

Below is a Positive Feedback Worksheet filled out by Lacie, a widowed respiratory therapist with two kids in grade school.

		Lacie's Positive Feedback Worksheet	
Age	**Person**	**Situation**	**Positive Feedback**
5	Mrs. DeAngelo	Parents day at school	Hugged me in front of mom, showed painting.
12	Sister Margaret Rose	Speech tournament	Praised my persuasive oratory piece.
14	Judy	Science day	Said I was best lab partner ever.
15	Mr. Delgado	Got behind in French class	Passed me anyway: "D for Determination."
15	Horace	Halloween party	Defended me to Jane.
18	Mother	Sorority rush week	Complimented me on being outgoing and organized.
19	Dr. Prescott	Chem lab	Said I had the mind of a true scientist.
19	Teachers	Second semester junior year	All A's on report card.
20	Jack	First true love	Broke up with Lorraine to go with me.
21	Father	Graduation	Showed up sober and said he was proud.
22	Roche interviewer	First medical job	Started me two levels higher than entry pay.
25	Denny	Favorite radio station	Had them play our song on my birthday.
26	Denny	Two ordinary days	Roses and candy.
27	Valerie at hospital	Understaffed	"I can always count on you."
29	Jackie D.	Daycare pickup	"You have such nice kids because you're nice yourself."
30	Guy at Sears	Buying microwave	"You really know what you're talking about."

My Positive Feedback Worksheet

Age	Person	Situation	Positive Feedback

Re-Evaluating the Negatives

To get a clearer picture of your core belief about self-worth, you need to identify the negative things you think about yourself in each area of your life. In the left column of the form below, list the negative traits you exhibit in eight different domains. Use the first words that come to mind, however harsh—the kind of critical judgments that you pass on yourself automatically.

When you have at least one negative statement for each domain, go back and rewrite the statements in positive form in column two. In rewriting your negative traits, follow these important guidelines:

- *Change Negative Terms to Neutral Terms.* Pejorative words like "lazy, weak, retarded, selfish" have got to go. Change "too lazy to work hard" to "tend to conserve energy." Change "selfish" to "preserve personal boundaries."

- *Use Accurate Language.* Temper all the exaggerations and embellishments in your negative statements. Absolute terms like "never" and "always" should be replaced with more accurate words such as "seldom" and "often." Confine yourself to the facts. Avoid extreme language like "I'm hopeless at all math" in favor of more accurate statements such as, "I confuse 8s and 3s" or "I forget the times tables past 8x8."

- *Replace General Terms with Specific Terms.* Make your re-evaluations fit each specific situation. Instead of "People walk all over me, I can't say no," write, "I find it hard to turn my sister down when she needs a babysitter." The general, "I'm a nonentity, I disappear in a crowd" should be rewritten as the more specific, "I feel shy in gatherings of more than four people whom I don't know."

- *Find Exceptions and Corresponding Strengths.* This is especially important in those areas where you feel very one-down, very less-than. For every weakness, there is a corresponding strength. For every vice, there is a virtue. For every lack in one place, there is an abundance elsewhere.

Example

Here is a Re-Evaluation Worksheet filled out by Jeanie, an antique shop owner who felt pushed around by her customers, her grown kids, and her husband.

Jeanie's Re-Evaluation Worksheet

Negative traits	Positive Re-evaluation
Emotional	
Feel shy and apologetic about my shop. Terrified by strong emotions in others.	*I'm a low-pressure saleswoman. Cautious around boisterous or angry people.*
Relationship	
Can't say no to Barbara or Joe, they push me around. Cave in to husband Ricky's every whim.	*Generous to the kids, give them latitude. Value peace and quiet over control. Did insist on going away last summer vacation*
Work/Career	
My "career" amounts to a junk pile. I'm too gutless to do anything different.	*I've made a respectable living. Many have found treasures in my shop. I'm conservative, stick with the tried and true. I did well with the retired Beanie Babies.*
Pleasure/Recreation	
I'm a Joanie one-note, go antiquing on vacation. I'm too weird to have fun.	*Antiques are my passion, so there. I enjoy special pleasures, like finding a first edition in a thrift store.*
Financial	
Hopeless with taxes, inventory, depreciation.	*I let the accountant do the books.*
Environment	
I'm spineless about getting Ricky to redecorate. I don't deserve nice things.	*Could be more assertive. I have nice things, although they're all in the store.*
Health/Energy Level	
My family has sucked the life out of me. I'd be better off dead.	*I've given much to my family. Sometimes feel depressed.*
Education/Knowledge	
Know everything about silver patterns, but nothing about life.	*I know a lot about antiques, and a little about life.*

My Re-Evaluation Worksheet

Negative traits	Positive Re-evaluation
Emotional	
Relationship	
Work/Career	
Pleasure/Recreation	
Financial	
Environment	
Health/Energy Level	
Education/Knowledge	

Putting It All Together

What have you learned so far? Review your Exceptions to the Rule Worksheet, your Positive Feedback Worksheet, and the Re-evaluation form you have just concluded. Have these exercises changed the way you think about your value as a human being? Has your core belief shifted or softened in some way? Go back to your Core Belief Worksheet now and review the words you used to describe your beliefs about self-worth. In the space below, rewrite that statement, incorporating what you know now about exceptions to the rule, positive feedback from others, and ways you can more accurately describe your weaknesses and strengths.

What's Your Belief—Revised

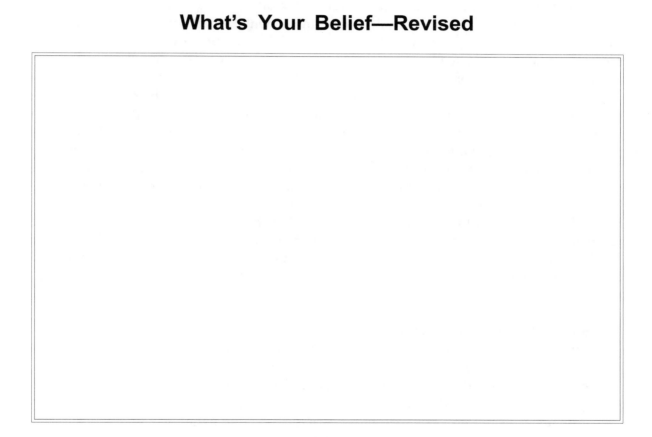

As you move on to more difficult, longer term problems, your core belief will give rise to feelings of shame and worthlessness. The rest of this chapter presents ways to cope with these feelings of shame when they arise.

Coping with Feelings of Shame

Coping with any negative feeling takes hard work and planning. And even then, the painful feelings won't entirely go away—they will just become more manageable. Coping with your feelings of shame is a five step process: 1.) Anchoring to Positive Memories, 2.) Preparing Coping Thoughts, 3.) Handling Negative Feedback, 4.) Designing a Coping Plan, and 5.) Making a Commitment.

Step 1. Anchoring to Positive Memories

Using this technique is simple. You dwell on a pleasant memory until you begin to feel good, then touch your wrist to "anchor" the memory and the feeling. After you do this with two or three positive memories, you will have created an instant stimulus (i.e., touching your wrist) that reliably brings about an instant response (i.e., feeling good about yourself).

You can do this exercise right now, sitting in your chair. Close your eyes, let your head droop forward, and relax by focusing on taking deep, slow breaths and releasing any muscular tension you feel in your body. Think back to a time in the past when you received positive feedback, felt loved and worthwhile, or achieved something you were proud of. When you find such a memory, relive it in all its sensory details—see what happened, hear the voices, feel the weather, sense movements, inhale smells. Make it as vivid as you can, until you begin to actually feel some of the well-being you associate with the memory. When you are feeling good in the memory, touch or tap or pinch your wrist in some distinctive way that you can repeat at will.

Repeat this process with another pleasant memory, intensifying the details until you feel good, then touching your wrist in the same way. If you have trouble thinking of good memories, return to your Exceptions to the Rule and Positive Feedback Worksheets for ideas. Go on and do the whole process with a third memory. By the third iteration, you will have established an automatic stimulus/response loop. Touching your wrist in the future when you're feeling worthless will be an automatic "anchor" to better times, allowing you to immediately access and recreate the good feeling from the past.

When Joyce tried this, she remembered the day she got her first kitten, the year she received her GED, and the time she volunteered at the hospital and felt needed. At the height of each memory she touched the two bony lumps on her wrist with her thumb and ring fingers. This became her "magic wand" gesture to dispel vague feelings of discomfort in groups and shame concerning her appearance.

Step 2. Preparing Coping Thoughts

When you feel worthless, it's easy to imagine situations in which you might be exposed as somehow inadequate, flawed, contemptible, or less worthwhile than others. So you avoid those kinds of situations you dread. The avoidance lessens the dread, makes you feel a little better, and reinforces the pattern of avoidance.

Researcher Donald Meichenbaum discovered that these patterns of avoidance can be changed by simple coping thoughts (1977). Coping thoughts are statements that remind you of evidence of your value and reassure you that you can make a difference in your world. Here are some coping thoughts that have helped others face their feelings of inadequacy:

I count in my kids' lives.

I have received honors for my volunteer work.

Remember Fanny when feeling small.

Many would miss me if I were gone.

I will live up to Dr. Gleason's opinion of me.

I have made a difference in my school.

Exercise

Notice that these statements tend to refer to past evidence of worth. This is the key to avoiding overwhelming feelings of shame in the present. Return to your Exceptions to the Rule and Positive Feedback Worksheets and mine them for material to use in writing your own coping thoughts here:

1. _____

2. _____

3. _____

4. _____

5. _____

Use your coping thoughts whenever the feelings of shame arise—when you approach an authority figure to make a request, when you need to assert your rights in your family, or when you are discouraged in solving a complicated financial problem that seems over your head.

When Rose had to ask a colleague not to smoke in their shared workplace, she used the coping thought, "I know how to take care of myself well." When she decided not to refinance her house and had to tell the pushy mortgage broker, she used the coping thought, "I deserve the same consideration as anybody." When her dog had cancer and she had to tell the vet to put her to sleep, she told herself, "I can make hard decisions like a grown up."

Step 3. Handling Negative Feedback

Just as sure as two plus two makes four, people always pursue what they perceive to be in their own best interest. The key word here is "perceive." You might not perceive that a drug-addicted teen's best interest dictates that he steal a TV and pawn it for money to buy crack; however, you can be sure that to the teen, at the time, given the circumstances and the resources at his disposal, that seems like the best option.

From this point of view, it is preposterous to torture yourself for past mistakes and shortcomings. It is equally unnecessary to agree with others who criticize you for past mistakes or offer any kind of negative feedback. Sure, from the vantage point of the present, with the 20/20 vision of hindsight, you may wish you had acted differently. But at the time, given your circumstances and the resources available to you, you did what you perceived to be in your self-interest. You did what seemed essential for your survival and well-being. You shouldn't have to cave in, apologize, and feel like scum over the fact that two plus two makes four.

This is the essence of handling negative feedback—to remind yourself and others that you are doing your best in each moment. To prove this to yourself, list three past mistakes or experiences that you tend to remember with shame. List the situation, what you did, and how you perceived your best interest.

Example

Below is a Best Interest Worksheet that was filled out by Fidelia, a twice divorced aide at a community health clinic.

Fidelia's Best Interest Worksheet

Situation	What I Did	Perceived Best Interest
Nursing school	Quit RN program	Seemed necessary to reduce stress, give time to earn money I needed right then
Bad marriage	Put up with Steve's abuse	Bruises healed, being alone felt fatal
Bad marriage #2	Stayed too long	Bird in the hand

My   Best Interest Worksheet

Situation	What I Did	Perceived Best Interest

Whenever someone criticizes you, remember this exercise. Stifle the urge to withdraw, argue, apologize, explain, justify, rationalize, grovel, or whatever. Instead, respond with one of these all-purpose comebacks that you have memorized for the occasion:

I was doing my best at the time.

That seemed like the best choice available to me.

Given the situation, I couldn't have done anything else.

Today I might be more clever, but then I was in survival mode.

(Your version) _____

Step 4. Designing a Coping Plan

This is where you put all three methods of coping with shame together into one plan, a response strategy that you can rehearse and apply in the future when the shameful feelings come up. Fill out the form below with your three anchoring memories, your five best coping thoughts, and your all-purpose response to negative feedback.

My Coping Plan

Anchors to good memories: When shame arises, I touch my wrist in a special way to remind me of

Good memory #1 _____

Good memory #2 _____

Good memory #3 _____

While enjoying the rush of remembered well-being, I recite one or two of my best coping thoughts:

Coping thought #1 _____

Coping thought #2 _____

Coping thought #3 _____

Coping thought #4 _____

Coping thought #5 _____

If anyone criticizes me, I stifle my feelings and recite my:

Response to negative criticism: _____

Example

Here is the Coping Plan prepared by Raymond, an electrician who lived alone and had recurring bouts of depression.

Raymond's Coping Plan

Anchors to good memories: When shame arises, I touch my wrist in a special way to remind me of

        Good memory #1 *Mom taking care of me when I had appendicitis*

        Good memory #2 *Listening to Julie sing* Greensleeves

        Good memory #3 *Cuddling with Amelie*

While enjoying the rush of remembered well-being, I recite one or two of my best coping thoughts:

        Coping thought #1 *My mother loved me and loves me still*

        Coping thought #2 *I have a keen appreciation of art and design*

        Coping thought #3 *When the chips are down I can be counted on*

        Coping thought #4 *I keep my word*

        Coping thought #5 *I really care for people*

If anyone criticizes me, I stifle my feelings and recite my:

        Response to negative criticism: *I always do what seems right at the time*

You might want to write your coping plan small on an index card or other conveniently sized piece of paper that you can carry with you in your purse or wallet. Seeing it from time to time will remind you that you have a prepared way to cope with feelings of shame, and allow you to rehearse your coping response so that it becomes second nature.

When you mentally rehearse your coping plan, imagine yourself successfully applying it in the worst situation that could happen. Make up a nightmare scenario in which your worst fears about self-worth would come true. Then imagine yourself rallying, using your coping plan, and handling the feelings of shame better than you ever have before.

Raymond's worst case scenario was showing up on a job site for final inspection of the wiring and having the building inspector excoriate him for some stupid, dangerous, bonehead mistake like forgetting to ground the main power box. He imagined himself flushing, his head lowering, his knees quivering, feeling speechless and ashamed. Then he pretended that he remembered his coping plan—touched his wrist, recited a couple of coping thoughts, and responded with a version of his all-purpose response to negative criticism: "I obviously didn't omit the ground wire on purpose. When I checked this box the other day, it seemed right at the time, but I missed that one detail." He imagined the inspector smiling good-naturedly and saying, "Well, that's why we have this last inspection. No harm done."

5. Making a Commitment

Your coping plan will work by buffering you from feelings of shame, buying you time in which to cope with and lessen the flood of feeling, so that you can go on with solving problems and making changes in your life. However, your coping plan will work only if you remember it and put it into practice.

Therefore, commit to yourself, and to someone you trust, to use your coping plan and to apply the problem-solving steps in this book. We call the person you commit to the "motivator." Explain to the motivator that you are learning better problem-solving techniques, and that you need help staying on track and overcoming your doubts about your self-worth.

Ask the motivator to check in with you at least once a week to monitor your progress. Research shows that making this kind of commitment to someone else is very effective in increasing motivation and follow through for all kinds of behavior change goals. Talk to your motivator often to report progress and discuss your experiences.

4

The Core Belief of Safety

The belief that it's dangerous to try new things can hugely inhibit problem solving. This chapter is about (1) recognizing how this belief stops you from attempting new solutions, and (2) challenging the belief so you are set free to tackle important life problems. The first step is to *map* the structure and impact of your core belief.

Mapping Your Core Belief

In a few pages you'll find a blank Core Belief Worksheet. It will help you explore the belief that trying to change or do something new is dangerous. The first question on the worksheet is, "What's your belief?" Write in your own words what you believe about the dangers of changing or doing new things. What kind of dangerous or threatening things could happen if you attempt to learn or do something new? Right now, in that section of your worksheet, put a description of what you *think* will happen if you try new problem-solving solutions.

An insurance salesman, who wanted to return to school, wrote this: "Basically, I believe that if I take a risk, it'll end in disaster. In this case, my family will get angry at me and it'll be a financial horror; I won't be able to find a new job."

The second question on the worksheet is, "What feelings does it bring?" Write down your emotional reaction when you try something that feels risky or dangerous. One feeling will almost certainly be fear. But there may be other feelings like sadness, a sense of helplessness, or frustration.

An advertising executive, who was trying to cut down her work hours, wrote this: "The whole time I'm going to be terrified that they'll use my reduced hours as an excuse to lay me off. And I'll probably get depressed about the inevitability of losing my job."

The third question on the worksheet is, "Where does it come from?" You should write down all the early messages from parents and other family members about how risky and dangerous life is, particularly when you try to change or do something new.

A church pastor, who wanted to do something about squabbling in the parish, thought of things his mother used to say: "Watch out for people, they'll always find a way to screw you. Don't make yourself a target." He also thought about how she went into a rage when he asked her to protect him from his father's beatings.

The fourth question is, "What are the triggers?" Under this question is a list of eight key arenas for you to explore. Ask yourself the following questions. What emotions trigger my core belief that it's dangerous to change or try new things? What changes have I tried to make in my relationships that made me feel unsafe? What changes have I tried to make at work that made me feel at risk, and so on? Try to fill in as much as you can think of for each arena. Use a separate page if you need to.

The fifth question on the worksheet is, "What are your compensating behaviors?" This is an opportunity to explore what you do when you start feeling afraid. How do you cope when you want to make a change but feel scared that something bad might happen? Compensating behaviors for the fear of change often involve avoidance, rationalizing that it wouldn't work anyway, trying to get others to take the risk for you, and bitter complaining.

Example

This Core Belief Worksheet was filled out by Charlene, a homemaker who wanted to start a mail order business to improve her finances. A core belief that trying new things is dangerous made her reluctant even to take the first step of product development.

Charlene's Core Belief Worksheet

What's your belief (in your own words)?

Whatever I try will come back to bite me. With the mail order business I'll lose all the money we put into development costs and really screw up our finances. And all the advertising will be an expensive waste. It'll be a disaster.

What feeling does it bring?

Anxiety; guilt that I'll make our family problems worse.

Where does it come from (in your family of origin)?

Every time I tried something as a kid, every time I took any risk, my father would warn me of all the ways it could end in disaster. Like when I ran for school president and he said I'd make all my friends jealous and they'd be cold to me.

What are the triggers?

Emotions: *Mostly feelings of anxiety. Also, when I get angry about something and want to change it.*

Relationships: *Every time John complains about something and I think I ought to do something to solve it, I get anxious.*

Work/Career: *Every job I've ever had I've worried about losing; every time I was assigned to do something new, I'd worry that something I hadn't thought of would go wrong.*

Education/Knowledge: *I often worry that I don't know something I really need to know.*

Money: *Any risk I take with money makes me expect to lose everything.*

Recreation/Pleasure: *Very anxious about planning vacations, particularly to a new place. Fear of getting ripped off, or getting a lousy hotel, or getting mugged in a strange town where we don't know the bad neighborhoods.*

Environment: *New places.*

Health: *If I have to deal with some new symptom or health problem, I always assume I have cancer.*

What are your compensating behaviors for:

Emotional triggers: *If I'm anxious, I try to push someone else to make changes or fix things. But they never do, and I end up feeling helpless.*

Relationship triggers: *I advise John about all the things he should do to fix something, but I rarely do anything myself.*

Work/Career triggers: *Be nice, nice, nice. Don't volunteer for anything. Avoid challenges.*

Education/Knowledge triggers? *Ask people for advice, rather than learning things on my own.*

Money triggers? *Let John make all money decisions; take no risks.*

Recreation/Pleasure triggers? *Let John plan vacations, which means we go nowhere.*

Environment triggers? *Don't go anywhere new—avoid.*

Health triggers? *Call the doctor all the time and get expensive tests. Which makes me hate myself because I'm wasting money.*

It's Your Turn

Below is the actual worksheet you've been learning how to fill out. If you're not sure what to do in a particular section, go back to the example worksheet and try to use that as a model. Remember, this is an opportunity to get at the root of what's keeping you stuck, so it's important to be honest with your answers.

My Core Belief Worksheet

What is your belief (in your own words)?

What feelings does it bring?

Where does it come from (in your family of origin)?

What are the triggers:

Emotions:

Relationships:

Work/Career:

Education/knowledge:

Money:

Recreation/Pleasure:

Environment:

Health:

What are your compensating behaviors for:

Emotional triggers?

Relationship triggers?

Work/Career triggers?

Education/Knowledge triggers?

Money triggers?

Recreation/pleasure triggers?

Environment triggers?

Health triggers?

How Your Core Belief Influences Problem Solving

Now it's time to look at some of the specific problems that you want to solve, and identify how your core belief regarding safety has been blocking you. You are reading this book for a very important reason—there are things you need to change in your life. In the left-hand column of the worksheet below, write down at least three problems you've struggled (but failed) to solve in the past few years.

You've learned something about compensating behaviors from the Core Beliefs Worksheet you just completed. Now you have a chance to examine specific ways they may have sabotaged your problem-solving efforts. Did you find yourself avoiding when you needed to work at your new solution? Did you take the first step toward attacking the problem, and then give up? Did you try to get someone else to solve it for you? Whatever compensating behaviors you may have used, describe them in the right-hand column of the worksheet below. Remember that compensating behaviors are a way to cope with your core belief about safety—the feeling that it's dangerous to attempt change or to try new things. If you need help to recognize compensating behaviors, return to the filled-in example of the Core Beliefs Worksheet and check out the section on compensating behaviors you'll find there.

Example

Here's a filled out Problem-Solving Worksheet by Carl to give you an idea of how to do this exercise. Notice that the column headed "Problems You've Attempted to Solve" includes both a description of the problem as well as an attempted solution.

Carl's Problem-Solving Worksheet	
Problems You've Attempted to Solve	**Compensating Behaviors**
1. Want to retire; trying to sell the barber shop.	1. Wrote an ad, but didn't call it in to the paper. 2. Ran the retirement numbers, but can't remember to discuss them with Dorrie (wife). 3. I tell customers I'm tired of being a barber.
2. Dorrie wants my miniature train layout out of the spare bedroom; look for alternative space.	1. Talked to next-door neighbor about renting his garage, but didn't follow up. 2. Avoid going into "train room" so Dorrie won't think about it.
3. Flooded basement; need to get contractor.	1. Called two or three contractors, but made no appointments. 2. Stonewall, or get angry, when Dorrie complains about it.
4. Need cash; trying to sell five acres outside of Forestville.	1. Called a couple of agents, but made no commitment to sell. 2. Got angry when Dorrie pressured me. 3. Finally, listed the property. Sold for below market value so I didn't have to worry about it anymore.
5. Mother in nursing home; need to get cash from her estate.	1. Tried to get my brother to do it. 2. Called a lawyer; canceled appointment.
6. Dorrie and I decided we need a vacation.	1. Saw a travel agent and got lots of brochures. Stuck them somewhere and lost track of them. 2. Talked about Puerto Vallarta, but didn't call to get info.

Problem-Solving Worksheet

Problems You've Attempted to Solve	Compensating Behaviors
1.	1. 2. 3.
2.	1. 2. 3.
3.	1. 2. 3.
4.	1. 2. 3.
5.	1. 2. 3.
6.	1. 2. 3.

Using What You've Learned

The belief that you're not safe, that there is danger in trying new things, triggers compensating behaviors. These behaviors help you avoid anxiety, but your problems never get solved. Change continues to feel dangerous because you never challenge the core belief. In fact, *avoidance reinforces the belief because it maintains the illusion that change is a dangerous thing.*

From now on, you need to monitor all your problem-solving efforts, watching for the first sign of your old, compensating behaviors. Then stop them. Immediately. And replace them with the coping plan you'll develop later in this chapter. The key is vigilance—not letting the compensating behaviors really get started.

Testing Your Core Belief

Anxiety really is a combination of two things: (1) the perception of risk, that something bad is likely to happen, and (2) your sense of how well you could cope in a worst case scenario. Testing and evaluating your core beliefs regarding safety requires that we look at both these components.

Trying to Change Is Dangerous—Bad Things Are Likely to Happen

How true is this? If you believe what your gut tells you, it may seem very true. Your anxiety, when facing change or novel situations, may feel like proof positive that you're taking a big risk. Right now we're going to examine this belief, and find out how true it really is across your entire life experience. To do this, we'll use an exercise called the "Evidence Log."

The Evidence Log Worksheet has three columns. In the left-hand column, you'll list all the evidence from your past that supports the belief that change is dangerous—that bad things are likely to happen. Think back over your entire life, and write down times when a new or changing situation turned out to have very negative consequences. In the middle column, you'll write evidence from your past experience that actually contradicts this belief. Here you would list times when you tried something new, or something new was thrust on you, and the outcome was positive. In the right-hand column of the worksheet, after thoroughly exploring evidence for and against your belief, you should write a balancing or alternative thought that takes into account your whole life experience. The belief that change is dangerous may soften or shift somewhat as you fully explore the evidence.

Example

The following Evidence Log was completed by Glenn, a forty-two-year-old computer programmer who was very cautious about making changes and taking risks.

Glenn's Evidence Log

Evidence For	Evidence Against	Balancing or Alternative Thought
Transferred to a new school. Got beaten up a lot the first year.	Started the chess club; nice experience, met friends.	While I've made some mistakes that hurt me, or where bad things happened, I've made a lot of changes and tried things that really did work out (Ann, most of my jobs, investments, computer school, etc.). In my life, change has more often been good than bad.
I joined the tennis team in school. Tore meniscus in knee.	Most of my jobs have turned out okay. Met Ann at a barbeque, pursued her, it worked out.	
Left Laura for someone I thought was better—but the new girl decided I didn't have enough ambition. Rejected.	Trip to Europe was good, except falling into canal in Venice.	
Moved to the apartment on Geary St.—horrible traffic noise, car stolen.	Bet that the stock market would go down—did well during dot.com crash.	
Transferred to the testing laboratory at the refinery. Chemical fumes caused me to get dizzy. Had to quit.	Forced to tackle big computer problem at work—and basically solved it.	
Vacation to Mazatlan. Got the "touristas" and spent most of the time in the bathroom.	Found good assisted living facility for my grandmother.	
	Found my sister a job.	
	Went back to school in programming—was good at it.	

Now it's time for you to get to work and fill out your own Evidence Log for the belief that change is dangerous. Mine all of your past experience for evidence on both sides of the question. Try to be as complete and honest with yourself as possible. When you've finished collecting evidence, read it over and write a balancing or alternative thought that reflects the evidence.

My Evidence Log		
Evidence For	**Evidence Against**	**Balancing or Alternative Thought**

If Something Bad Happens,
I Won't Be Able to Cope

This belief is a cornerstone of anxiety because it implies you're not equipped to face challenging situations. But is this true? If you reviewed your entire life history, are there absolutely no times when you rose to face a challenging or difficult situation?

We'll explore this question with the Evidence Log Worksheet you've just gotten familiar with. In the left-hand column, you'll be looking through your past experience for evidence that supports the idea that you can't cope when bad things happen. In the middle column, you'll write evidence from your past—specific situations—where you did cope reasonably well with a crisis or serious problem. Finally, in the right-hand column, you'll write a balanced or alternative thought based on all the evidence you've collected.

Example

The following Evidence Log was filled out by Barbara, a fifty-one-year-old legal assistant.

Barbara's Evidence Log		
Evidence For	**Evidence Against**	**Balancing or Alternative Thought**
Fell apart when I went to high school. Depressed and alone. Couldn't figure out how to make friends.	Was a big support to Bill when his father died.	There have been several situations where I got so anxious that I didn't cope well— particularly when I was younger. But actually I've handled a lot of problems and setbacks over the years and did okay. I do better when I have time to prepare myself to face something.
When Bill (husband) lost his job, got very anxious about everything and didn't cope well. Kids complained I was "out of it."	Handled a lot of statute deadlines and crises as a legal assistant.	
New office manager at work. Felt criticized all the time, couldn't take it. Quit.	Coped pretty well when I had the carpal tunnel problem and required surgery.	
Bobby (son) had that back injury playing soccer. Couldn't deal with the hospital, the doctors. Had to let Bill handle it.	Found and coordinated the professional help we got to deal with Bobby's learning disability.	
	Stood up to next-door neighbor who was threatening to sue us.	
	Ice storm and two day power loss. Coped well with that.	
	Bill angry about money— eventually faced him about it and worked out agreement.	
	Did well when we had to move—made two new friends.	

Now it's your turn to fill in the Evidence Log. Remember, you're looking for evidence both for and against the belief that you can't cope with problems or crises. Go ahead and complete your Evidence Log with as may situations or decisions that you can remember from your past.

My Evidence Log		
Evidence For	**Evidence Against**	**Balancing or Alternative Thought**

Testing Your Core Belief on Real Problem Solving

Right now we'd like you to choose a problem you would like to use this workbook to solve. It can regard any domain of your life. There may be one or two solutions you've considered for the problem, but have felt afraid to implement them. Your core belief about the danger of trying something new made it very hard to forge ahead. Now we're going to introduce an exercise to help you make a better assessment of the actual danger in any new solution you consider. It's called the Risk Assessment Worksheet.

The Risk Assessment Worksheet starts with a question about the *worst possible outcome* if you tried your new solution. Then you *rate the probability* that the worst would happen. After that, you explore *how you would cope*, in the event of the worst outcome. There's a space here for coping actions—things you'd do to manage or survive a bad situation—and coping thoughts that would keep your head on straight. Typical coping thoughts remind you that you've gotten through similar situations in the past, that the difficulty will be time limited, that even the darkest cloud may have a silver lining, and that you have resources and support to help you through.

The next section of the Risk Assessment Worksheet is a *revised prediction* of the worst outcome. After exploring possible coping actions and coping thoughts, you may see the worst case scenario somewhat less bleakly. You may now have a sense that you'd come out of it and recover, no matter how difficult the initial struggle. The next section of the worksheet looks at *evidence against the worst possible outcome*. This is similar to the work you've done on the Evidence Log. You list all the facts and circumstances that make you suspect that things won't go as badly as you fear. The next section of the worksheet explores alternative and more likely outcomes. Here you list as many possible outcomes as you can think of to your new solution. They don't have to all be positive, but none will be as bad as the worst case scenario. The last step in the Risk Assessment Worksheet is to re-rate the probability that the worst case scenario will, indeed, occur. For most people, after conscientiously working through the Risk Assessment Worksheet, the worst case outcome seems less probable.

Example

The following Risk Assessment Worksheet was filled out by Carey, a twenty-eight-year-old woman who'd been sexually abused as a child, and was now having symptoms of Post-Traumatic Stress Disorder when she attempted to have intercourse with her boyfriend. The solution she's exploring in the worksheet is a proposal that they go to couples therapy to work on the sexual problem there.

Carey's Risk Assessment Worksheet

What bad thing might happen—worst case scenario?

Once we got our sexual issues out in the open with a therapist, Steve might get so angry and frustrated that he gives up on the relationship. He might decide that the whole thing's impossible—I'm impossible—and walk out. I'd be totally devastated.

Rate probability: *50%* chance.

How would I cope?

Coping actions: *I'd move in with my girlfriend, Julie. I'd continue working on my sexual problems in individual therapy. I'd spend more time doing music with my friends, and get support while I'm grieving about Steve. I might go back to school and get my teaching credential to have something positive to focus on.*

Coping thoughts: *I'd tell myself that I'll get through it, I'll recover. I'd remind myself that I'd gotten over other losses. Also, I'd try to recognize that if Steve didn't care about me enough to work together on our sexual problems, then he really was the wrong partner for me. And I'm glad to know now rather than five years and two kids later. I'd tell myself that Julie and my friends won't let me fall apart.*

Revised prediction of worst outcome:

I'd be sad, angry. I'd have a hard several months. But I'd do things to take care of myself, and I have a good support network. I wouldn't be totally devastated.

Evidence against worst possible outcome:

- *I think Steve wants to stay together—he's always said that.*
- *Steve seemed somewhat positive about my idea of going to therapy.*
- *We still have some ways of being sexual together—I try to do things that I can tolerate.*
- *He tells me he loves me.*
- *We've solved other problems together—like his complaint that I seemed preoccupied and busy most evenings; and my dislike of his idiot friend, Levin.*

Alternative (more likely) outcomes:

- *Our sexual relationship will get somewhat better, but we still won't be able to do certain things.*
- *We might find some new ways to please each other.*
- *We might quit therapy and let the whole thing go underground again.*
- *Steve might get angry and frustrated, but continue talking and working on it.*
- *We might agree to put off any rash decisions about our relationship until I'd done six months or a year worth of individual therapy to deal with the abuse trauma.*

Re-rate probability: *20%* chance.

What happened when I tried the new solution?

Now try this one yourself. Identify a solution to a problem that you've put off out of fear. Start by writing in the worst case scenario, and then filling in the remaining items of the worksheet. If you have trouble thinking of coping thoughts, go to a later section in this chapter called "Using Coping Thoughts." The example Risk Assessment Worksheet may also help you if you have trouble with any of the items.

My Risk Assessment Worksheet

What bad thing might happen—worst case scenario?

Rate probability: ____% chance.

How would I cope:
Coping actions:

Coping thoughts?

Revised prediction of worst case outcome:

Evidence against worst possible outcome:

Alternative (more likely) outcomes:

Re-rate probability: ____% chance.

What happened when I tried the new solution?

Looking at Outcomes

You probably noticed on the bottom of the Risk Assessment Worksheet a question that asks, "What happened when I tried the new solution?" This is something you should fill out when you've actually attempted the solution on which your Risk Assessment Worksheet is based. Looking at the actual outcome is a very important way of testing your core belief. If the outcome is less painful than your worst case scenario, then it suggests you may be "over-predicting" catastrophe. And this is good evidence that your core belief about safety needs to be revised.

Each time you do a Risk Assessment Worksheet that leads to actual problem solving, be sure to go back and answer that last question. The more you encounter the gap between the nightmare outcome you expect and reality, the more success you'll have at overcoming the inhibiting effects of your core belief.

Putting It All Together

What have you learned so far? After reviewing your Evidence Logs and Risk Assessment Worksheet, is there anything new in how you think about the danger of attempting novel solutions? Is your core belief softening? Is there any way it has altered, after doing these exercises? Go back to your Core Belief Worksheet now and read the words you used to describe your belief about safety. In the space that follows rewrite that statement. Incorporate some of your balanced or alternative thoughts, as well as what you've learned through your risk assessment.

What's Your Belief—Revised

Coping with Fear (Without Compensating Behaviors)

Coping with any fear takes work. And planning. Even then, the fear won't completely disappear—it will just be more manageable. Coping with the fear of trying new things requires four steps:

1. learning to relax in the face of the fear,

2. learning to replace "what if" thoughts with coping thoughts,

3. making a coping plan, and

4. making a *commitment* to cope rather than avoid.

Learning to Relax

When you feel anxious about your capacity to try something new, when thoughts of catastrophe pressure you to avoid a challenge, physical relaxation can help. The quickest, and arguably the best, relaxation technique available is cue controlled relaxation. It's easy to learn, and the effects are every bit as powerful as a dose of Xanax.

The four steps to learning cue controlled relaxation are:

1. learning to take a deep, diaphragmatic breath,

2. selecting a cue word,

3. imagining a "moving band," and

4. practicing cue controlled breathing. All four of these steps are explained in detail in Chapter 2, "The Core Belief of Competence," under the section, "Learning to Relax."

Using Coping Thoughts

Researcher Donald Meichenbaum discovered that we can inoculate ourselves against fear with surprisingly simple coping thoughts (1977). The idea is to replace thoughts of catastrophe and danger with more realistic thinking. Here are some examples of coping statements that have helped people face anxiety related to changing and doing new things:

- Just because I'm anxious doesn't mean anything bad will happen. It's just a feeling I can cope with.

- The odds are against anything bad happening.

- I can be anxious and still do what I need to do.

- I can relax and get through this.

- I can ride this through—I don't need to let this get to me.

- I won't let negative thoughts run away with me—just keep focused on the task.

- Nothing serious is going to happen to me.

- I'm trying something new, but I can handle it.

- These are just scary thoughts, not reality.

- I'll do my best, that's all anyone can ask of me.

- Things don't have to go perfectly. I can cope with glitches and mistakes.

- This anxiety won't hurt me—it just doesn't feel good.

- Avoiding doesn't solve anything—I'm going to deal with this now.

- Disasters are rare—I'll keep forging ahead.

- I can cope with whatever happens.

- If there are new problems, I'll get through them.

- Fear won't defeat me. I can do this.

Coping statements like these can literally block out negative, "what if" thinking that focuses on all the things that can go wrong. Coping thoughts can calm you down and bring your attention back to the task at hand.

You may find that the generic coping thoughts we've listed above aren't quite right for you. That's okay. It's easy to write your own. Think of the problem-solving challenge you face. What could you say to yourself to make it less scary? For example, do you have skills that increase your chances for success? Do you have a plan to handle things if any of the problems you fear should occur? What are the odds that a serious problem might occur? Have you succeeded at a similar situation before? Do you have someone who will support and help you? Is there something you might enjoy about the challenge—no matter what happens? Coping thoughts should offer comfort—either the hope that you can succeed, or an affirmation that you can face the fear and the challenge, regardless of the outcome.

In the space below, write four of your own coping thoughts that might help you with the fear of trying something new:

_____

_____

_____

_____

Here's an example of how coping thoughts helped Arnold, who was trying to problem solve regarding his teenage son's drug abuse. After much thought, and research into treatment alternatives, he decided that his boy needed a family intervention, followed by placement in an inpatient treatment program.

This plan triggered a lot of fear and catastrophic thinking. What if the intervention so alienated his son that Arnold lost all relationship to the boy? What if the treatment program encouraged him to blame things on the family? What if they spent thousands of dollars and he went back to drugs anyway? What if his son ran away to live on the streets rather than go into treatment? The possibilities for disaster seemed endless.

To combat the anxiety set off by these scenarios, Arnold chose coping thoughts that seemed helpful—and repeated them to himself each time the "what ifs" came up. "I can be anxious and still do what I need to do," he said to himself. And, "I'll do my best, that's all anyone can do." And, "Avoiding will make things worse—I have a good plan to deal with this." And finally, "Fear can't stop me from doing what my boy needs—I'll cope with whatever happens."

Notice that Arnold didn't try to refute his catastrophic thoughts. Instead he just affirmed that he could do what he needed to do *despite* his fear. And that he could deal with whatever happened. The whole point of coping thoughts is to remind you that you possess the strength and resiliency to face a challenge, and no setback is going to be irreparable.

How a Coping Plan Can Fight Fear

Making a coping plan is like saving money for a rainy day. It helps you weather the hard times when you're hit by fears and unexpected problems. A good coping plan helps you control the fear of catastrophe in three ways. First, you use relaxation skills to lower your anxiety—particularly when you're getting hit by "what if" thoughts, full of dangerous possibilities. Second, you choose three or four good coping statements to replace those scary, catastrophic thoughts. Third, you plan an alternative behavioral response to replace avoidance. This might include things like (a) making an appointment with yourself to do the next step of problem solving, (b) calling someone for support, (c) promising yourself a specific reward for finishing the next step of problem solving, (d) taking a brief rest break, with a set time for returning to a problem-solving task, (e) turning off the TV, the computer game, and all other avoidance activities, and (f) going to a place where you can focus exclusively on your problem-solving task.

When the "what if" worries start, and you begin to feel like giving up or avoiding a new challenge, immediately put your coping plan into action.

Example

Arnold photocopied the coping plan and filled in his four coping statements, previously mentioned. Then he did a lot of thinking about how his fears made him avoid planning the intervention for his son. He hadn't really decided on which inpatient program was best—he needed to tour several of them. And he also needed to find out about insurance. Most difficult was talking to relatives and friends, and setting a date with them for the intervention.

Typical avoidance strategies involved surfing the Internet, endless cable television, calling some buddies up for tennis, lying to himself that his son didn't look so stoned lately, questioning his son about drug activities (but accepting his false reassurances), and going places with his daughter while avoiding his son altogether.

Here is Arnold's list of coping behaviors to overcome fear-driven procrastination:

1. Go to my "to do" list for planning the intervention, and set a time, before the day is over, to do one thing.

2. Tell my wife I'm stalling, and promise to do something specific within the next 24 hours. Then report back to her.

3. Turn off all distractions (TV, computer) and get busy right now.

4. Ask my wife to sit with me for support while I make calls to family/friends, asking them to participate.

As it turned out, what helped Arnold most was being certain to do his coping behavior *on the same day* that he felt anxious and noticed the impulse to avoid.

My Coping Plan

1. Do three minutes of cue controlled relaxation to physically calm yourself down.

2. As soon as your body is relaxed, review your coping thoughts. Write them here:

_____

_____

_____

_____

Each time a negative, "what if " thought enters your mind, immediately replace it with a coping statement. Continue doing this until the anxiety abates.

3. The impulse to give up or avoid your problem-solving steps will be managed with at least one of the following four coping behaviors. Write them here:

_____

_____

_____

_____

The coping behavior *must* occur on the same day that you felt the anxiety. Any delay will reinforce avoidance.

Making a Commitment

Your coping plan will work—only if you do it. And you'll successfully manage your "what if" fears, but only if you follow your coping plan. Commit to yourself—and someone whose opinion matters to you—that you'll follow your coping plan for the next thirty days.

We call the person you commit to the "motivator." Explain to the motivator which problem-solving steps you've decided to take. Give them a copy of your coping plan to manage anxiety and stay focused on problem solving. This is the most important factor: ask the motivator to check in with you at least once per week to monitor your progress.

Research shows that commitments to others are more effective than private decisions at changing behaviors. While commitments to yourself can be forgotten or put off, it's embarrassing to have to explain to someone you respect why you are avoiding important goals. Take advantage of this fact. Get the motivator involved, and check in with him or her often about your problem-solving efforts.

5

The Core Belief
of Primacy

This is the belief that your needs are less important than the needs of others. If you were to put your own needs first, the Core Belief of Primacy predicts one or more of the following outcomes:

1. The other person will suffer uncontrollably because of you.

2. The other person won't be able to take adequate care of themselves without your help.

3. The other person will see you as bad, wrong, and selfish—and reject you.

4. You will end up despising yourself for being selfish and bad.

This chapter is about (1) recognizing how this belief limits your ability to solve problems, and (2) challenging the belief so you are freer to make important changes in your life. The first step is to *map* the structure and impact of your core belief.

Mapping Your Core Belief

In a few pages you'll find an exercise called the Core Belief Worksheet. It will help you explore the impact of your beliefs about primacy. The first question on the worksheet is, "What's your belief?" Write in your own words what you believe about the relative importance of your needs versus the needs of others. What do you think will happen if you attempted to solve a problem by putting your own needs first? Which of the four outcomes outlined above would you expect to happen?

A restaurant manager, who wanted to stop working weekends, was concerned about how other employees would feel if they were asked to work in his place on Saturday or Sunday. "You've got to take care of people," he wrote. "If you don't, they're going to think you're thoughtless, that all you care about is you. They'll probably quit, and I'll feel like I really screwed up."

The second question on the worksheet is, "What feelings does it bring?" Write down your emotional reaction when you're tempted to choose your own needs over the needs of others. Do you feel guilty, scared, ashamed, wrong, selfish, paralyzed?

A technical writer wanted to get more training in job-relevant software, but her boyfriend was pushing her to forget school and spend the weekends skiing with him. Her emotional reaction was guilt and a sense of doing something really bad. She also felt scared that her boyfriend would eventually leave her if she followed her needs and had less time for him.

The third question on the worksheet is, "Where does it come from?" Here you should write in early experiences with parents and other family members that made you doubt the importance of your own needs. Also write down negative things that were said to you when you attempted to do something for yourself.

A man, who frequently deferred to his wife's vacation preference over his own desires, remembered his father sending him away from the dinner table with the words, "Good-bye, big shot. Get out of here if all you're gonna think about is yourself. You're just a big *I am*."

The fourth question is, "What are the triggers?" Under this question is a list of three types of conflicts that are likely to trigger your core belief, along with associated feelings of guilt and fear. Ask yourself these questions:

1. Are there times when you experience emotional pain that would only get better if you did something that conflicts with the needs of others?

2. Are there times when you have conflicts of desire with family, friends, or co-workers that trigger feelings of guilt or anxiety?

3. Do you have values conflicts with others that trigger fear or guilt when you push them to do what you consider right? Try to fill in as much as you can think of for each of these three arenas. Use a separate page if you need it.

The fifth question on the worksheet is, "What are your compensating behaviors?" This is an opportunity to explore how you cope when your emotional pain, your desires, or values put you in conflict with others. Compensating behaviors for subsequent feelings of guilt or fear may include attacking and blaming, avoiding, giving up, back-biting, ganging up or rallying your supporters against another person, and so on.

Example

This Core Belief Worksheet was filled out by Carla, a single mother and attorney whose seven-year-old doesn't want her to date. Her core belief that she has no right to disappoint someone she loves is the starting point of the worksheet.

Carla's Core Belief Worksheet

What's your belief (in your own words)?

I've no right to hurt or upset someone I love. I'll end up hating myself.

What feelings does it bring?

Guilt, anxiety, feelings of being bad or selfish.

Where does it come from (in your family of origin)?

My mother. She seemed upset every time I wanted to spend time with my friends. She didn't want to be left alone with my father, and she made me feel selfish for wanting to be on my own.

What are the triggers for:

Conflicts Due to Emotional Pain?

I get lonely and empty, and sometimes sexually frustrated. Then immediately I feel like a really bad person to want to go on dates and leave my boy.

Conflicts of Desire?

How to divide up the workload at the law office, how often to go see my mother, what we'll watch on television. Then there's bedtime—I feel selfish to have my boy go to bed early so I can rest; boring games—I hate myself for not wanting to play them with him; my crazy sister always calling for emotional support; my friend wanting to endlessly discuss legal cases when I just want to play racquet ball.

Values Conflicts?

How soon we return client calls at the law office, how much pro bono work we do, the expectation that children should finish all of their homework.

What are the compensating behaviors for:

Conflicts Due to Emotional Pain?

I get angry at my son and accuse him of being selfish and not wanting me to be happy. Or I just have another glass of wine and avoid the whole thing.

Conflicts of Desire?

Just give up and decide I'll never get what I want. Avoid. Get angry at my boy (to cover my feelings of being selfish) when there's conflict about the TV or bedtime.

Values Conflicts?

Back-biting at work; try to get friends to gang up against the people I don't agree with (because I'm afraid to stand up to them myself).

It's Your Turn

On this page is the actual worksheet you've been learning how to fill out. If you're not sure what to do in a particular section, go back to the example worksheet and try to use that as a model. Try to be as honest with yourself as possible.

My Core Belief Worksheet

What's your belief (in your own words)?

What feelings does it bring?

Where does it come from (in your family of origin)?

What are the triggers for:

Conflicts Due to Emotional Pain (when you're hurting and need to stop it)?

Conflicts of Desire (when you have different desires/preferences/wants from others)?

Values Conflicts (when you have different ethical/spiritual values about the right way to do things)?

What are the compensating behaviors for:

Conflicts Due to Emotional Pain?

Conflicts of Desire?

Values Conflicts?

How Your Core Belief Influences Problem Solving

Now it's time to look specifically at some of the problems you want to solve and see how your core belief regarding the primacy of others' needs has blocked you. You're reading this book for a reason. Some things in your life aren't working; they need to change. In the left-hand column of the worksheet below, write down at least three problems you've struggled (but failed) to solve in the past few years.

You've gotten some understanding of compensating behaviors from the Core Beliefs Worksheet you've just completed. These are things you do to manage the guilt and anxiety when your needs conflict with others. Now you have a chance to examine which compensating behaviors may have sabotaged your problem-solving efforts. Do you find yourself avoiding or getting angry or giving up when your desires conflict with those you love? Does the fear of conflict and putting your own needs first make you find fault with every possible solution? Whatever compensating behaviors you have used, describe them in the right-hand column in the worksheet below. Remember that compensating behaviors are a way to block feelings of guilt, anxiety that you'll be rejected, or the sense that you're wrong and bad. If you need help identifying compensating behaviors, return to the filled-in example of the Core Beliefs Worksheet and check out the section on compensating behaviors you'll find there.

Example

Here's a filled out Problem-Solving Worksheet by Tanya to give you a model of how to do this exercise. Notice that the column headed "Problems You've Attempted to Solve" includes both a description of the problem as well as an attempted solution.

Tanya's Problem-Solving Worksheet

Problems You've Attempted to Solve	Compensating Behaviors
1. John is writing a novel and never wants to do anything on the weekend. Suggested doing something outdoors for a few hours on Sat. and Sun. I feel I have no right to interrupt an artist at work.	1. Make snide comments about the novel. 2. Be passive-aggressive and not talk to him when he talks to me. 3. Avoid the issue so I don't have to worry that he'll be angry.
2. Too little foreplay. He says he's afraid he'll lose his erection when I ask him to slow down. Don't feel I can ask for anything that would reduce his sexual pleasure.	1. Complain to my friend, Sally, rather than bring the issue up again with him. 2. Avoid sexual situations. 3. If he shows sexual interest, either cook up a little fight or try to get it over quickly.
3. No money to ever take a vacation. John pours it all into his sailboat. He takes so much pleasure in it, I couldn't ask him to give it up.	1. Refuse to go on the boat. 2. Complain to Sally. 3. Got mad one night and told him that all sailors are self-indulgent jerks.

My Problem-Solving Worksheet

Problems You've Attempted to Solve	Compensating Behaviors
1.	1. 2. 3.
2.	1. 2. 3.
3.	1. 2. 3.
4.	1. 2. 3.
5.	1. 2. 3.
6.	1. 2. 3.

Using What You've Learned

The belief that your needs are less important than others', and the expectation that you'll feel guilty and afraid if you do something for yourself, pushes you to use compensating behaviors. Notice that compensating behaviors never solve the problem. They just give you some temporary relief from feeling stuck and helpless.

You're so afraid of guilt and rejection that problem-solving efforts seem very dangerous. The thought that people would be disappointed or upset feels too disturbing, too big a risk to take.

But the price you pay for the core belief of primacy is high. Nothing changes. Nothing improves. From now on, you need to monitor all your problem-solving efforts—watching for the first sign of your old compensating behaviors. Then stop them. Cold. And replace them with the coping strategies you'll learn later in this chapter. The key is vigilance. Don't let yourself return to that old pattern of avoiding, picking fights, giving up, and so on.

Testing Your Core Belief

How True Is Your Core Belief?

By their very nature, core beliefs are generalities. They reflect what is true sometimes—but not always. One way to test your core belief that other people's needs are more important is to explore what happened on those occasions when you broke the rule. In other words, what was the outcome when you did take care of yourself, even though it may have disappointed someone else? On the Evidence Log that follows, list every single experience you can think of where you put your needs above someone else's. These should be written in the left-hand column, where it says "Conflict or Problem Situation."

The rest of the Evidence Log consists of an evaluation of the outcomes:

What evidence is there for or against Prediction #1: *that the other person will suffer uncontrollably because of you?*

What evidence is there for Prediction #2: *that the other person won't be able to adequately care for themselves?*

What evidence is there for Prediction #3: *that the other person will see you as bad, wrong, and selfish—and reject you?*

What evidence is there for Prediction #4: *that you will end up despising yourself for being selfish and bad?*

Write the *actual* outcome regarding each of these four prediction in the appropriate column. Remember that outcomes extend beyond what happened in the first few weeks, or even months. Outcomes, as you'll see in the following sample Evidence Log, require taking the long view of years or even decades.

José's Evidence Log

Conflict or Problem Situation	Belief #1	Belief #2	Belief #3	Belief #4
1. I told my mother I was leaving home 3 months after my father died. She didn't want me to go.	She was sad and called me all the time for 3–4 months. She seemed more at peace after a while.	Not true. She started square dancing, joined a grief group, took a trip to Europe with her sister.	In the beginning she was angry and accused me of not caring, but later she apologized. We're still close.	I did feel horribly wrong and guilty for 3–4 months. It eased, and I realized how relieved I was to be on my own.
2. Joined hiking and camping club even though Sandra doesn't like the outdoors and refused to participate.	She was very unhappy that I'd go hiking on Saturday, and particularly if I camped overnight. Stayed kind of bitter about it even though she stopped complaining.	She got into photography and started spending a lot of time in the darkroom. She was pretty good at taking care of herself.	In the beginning, her message was that I was being selfish. But she never rejected me because I was camping.	I was anxious that it was going to ruin our relationship. But that passed in a month or so.
3. Went to Spain without my friend Carl. We always said we'd do it together, but he kept putting it off because he couldn't get his money together.	He was pissed and disappointed. But he recovered and we went to Brazil two years later.	It forced him to get serious about saving his money because he realized I wouldn't wait for him forever.	He accused me of breaking a promise; said I was wrong to do it. But he never rejected me.	I felt okay. I was having too good a time in Madrid.
4. Left Sandra. I was afraid she'd disintegrate.	A lot of tears; a lot of sad conversations. But she started dating almost immediately.	She went back to grad school and moved in with her best friend. She was okay.	She didn't talk to me for several months and she said I'd betrayed her and destroyed her ability to trust. She seems to have let go of that; we now meet for lunch sometimes.	Deep guilt. Felt like a rotten person for a month or two. Finally decided I'd done us both a favor; both happier now.

Now it's time for you to get to work on your own Evidence Log for the core belief that other people's needs have primacy. Mine all of your past experience for situations and conflicts in which you *broke this rule*. Then thoroughly explore the outcomes in terms of the four predictions. Try to be as honest with yourself as possible.

My Evidence Log				
Conflict or Problem Situation	**Belief #1**	**Belief #2**	**Belief #3**	**Belief #4**

Coming to Conclusions

When you've finished collecting evidence, it's time to synthesize it into conclusions regarding the four predictions.

Prediction #1—The other person will suffer uncontrollably because of you.

Based on the evidence, what is your conclusion about the truth of this prediction?

_____

_____

_____

Prediction #2—The other person won't be able to take adequate care of themselves without your help.

Based on the evidence, what is your conclusion about the truth of this prediction?

_____

_____

_____

Prediction #3—The other person will see you as bad, wrong, and selfish; and reject you.

Based on the evidence, what is your conclusion about the truth of this prediction?

_____

_____

_____

Prediction #4—You will end up despising yourself for being selfish and bad.

Based on the evidence, what is your conclusion about the truth of this prediction?

_____

_____

_____

Much of the time you'll find that the evidence doesn't point to a black or white conclusion. You may notice, for example, that people react in the beginning very much as the beliefs would predict. But over time, they recover, take care of themselves, and are more accepting of your decision to take care of yourself. So when you write your conclusion, make sure it takes account of all the outcomes—both immediate and long-term, both positive and negative.

Evidence from the Experience of Others

A second way to evaluate your core belief is to look beyond your own experience and evaluate what happens to others. Think about the people you know—friends, family, co-workers—who have chosen to take care of their own needs over someone else's. What are the outcomes in these situations? What happens in terms of the four predictions? The following Evidence Log is divided into three columns:

1. Who,

2. What They Did, and

3. Outcomes (the four predictions).

The following sample will give you an idea of how to fill this out.

Anne's Evidence Log—Others		
Who	**What They Did**	**Outcomes (the four predictions)**
Jude	Forcefully urged an ambivalent husband to consider having children.	They have two great kids and both seem happy with the decision.
Carlette	Decided to go to grad school even though Bill wanted her to keep working.	She got an MA in journalism and found a job with a national magazine in New York. Bill moved there with her, grousing all the way. But he seems to like all the Big Apple cultural stuff, and Carlette is making good money again.
Henry	Pushed to turn the guest room into an office. His partner, Larry, was upset that there'd be no room for Larry's mother when she came to visit.	Henry bought Larry a sofa bed—by way of compensation—and the whole thing blew over.
Chuck	Wanted the Japanese rock garden in front—which Linda absolutely hates.	She was snide and contemptuous at first. Last week I heard her say the bonsai were "kind of cute."
Laura	Wanted Roderick to quit a job that required him to travel all the time.	He was resentful and blaming because his new job bored him. Eventually became a consultant, but he still seems angry when the subject of his old job comes up.

Now it's time to fill out your own Evidence Log to explore the experiences of people you know who've put their needs first. When thinking about the outcomes, try to put down everything you know that's relevant to the four predictions.

My Evidence Log—Others		
Who	**What They Did**	**Outcomes (the four predictions)**

Putting It All Together

What have you learned so far? After reviewing your Evidence Logs, is there anything new in how you think about the Core Belief of Primacy? Is the belief that your needs are less important than the needs of others shifting or softening? Has the expectation that you'll feel guilt or fear if you put yourself first altered after doing these exercises? Now go back to your Core Belief Worksheet and read the words you used to describe your beliefs about primacy. In the space below rewrite that statement, incorporating some of your new conclusions about the four predictions, as well as the data you've gathered about the experiences of others.

What's Your Belief—Revised

Coping with Guilt and Fear
(Without Compensating Behaviors)

Let's start with this: every human being has the *obligation* to protect his or her mental and physical health. In terms of physical health, this means addressing your body's needs for sleep, good nutrition, exercise, and so on. Mental health is trickier—but the obligation is just as strong. You have important needs for stimulation, belonging, love, support, recreation/relaxation, beauty, sexual expression, and so on.

While your mental health needs are just as important as your physical needs, people with the core belief of primacy tend to downplay them in favor of the needs of others. They'd never dream of feeding their bodies French fries three times a day, but they are willing to live on emotional scraps and junk food, just so no one else will be disappointed or denied something they want.

You have a right and *obligation* to take care of yourself. Sometimes you can't meet your needs and the needs of others at the same time. You have to make a choice. It's okay *sometimes* to sacrifice, to put others first. But if you do that all the time, you'll grow psychologically malnourished. You'll wither. The following exercise will help you evaluate the strength and importance of your needs versus the needs of others—for one particular solution or decision you're considering.

Exercise

Identify a problem and proposed solution where your needs appear to conflict with the needs of others. In the left-hand column of the Needs Assessment exercise, list all the emotional consequences for you should you implement the solution/decision. In the right-hand column, list all the emotional consequences for other people affected by your proposed solution. Now assign weights ranging from minus 10 to plus 10 for each of the listed consequences. Minus 10 would represent the absolute worst pain you can imagine; plus 10 would be ecstasy. It's likely that many of your needs will get weights on the positive end of the scale because the proposed solution benefits you emotionally. Others' needs may sometimes be affected negatively. Make your best and most honest guess about how to assign these weights. Add the numbers up in each column to get an overall sense of how the proposed solution/decision affects you versus others.

Example

In the following example, Gloria was considering a move from the inner city to a small town. Here's how she did her needs assessment.

Gloria's Needs Assessment

The Problem: I hate Oakland, it's crowded and unsafe.

Proposed Solution/Decision: Move to a house owned by my brother-in-law in Grayton. Continue to work as a freelance editor—but do everything on-line.

How the Solution Affects:

	My Emotional Needs		Emotional Needs of Others
+7	Feel physically safer.	−7	Kids lose their friends in Oakland, have to adjust to new environment.
+2	More relaxed pace of life.		
+6	Worry less about the kids' risks at school.	−6	Kids' dad has to commute sixty miles to see them. May diminish contact with their dad.
−4	More lonely at first.	+2	Kids wouldn't have to bus to school.
+6	More of a sense of community in Grayton, ultimately could get more support from sister, neighbors, and friends.	−5	Grandparents would miss seeing the kids all the time.
−2	Hate driving—would have to drive kids to Oakland to see their dad and visit grandparents.	+4	My sister in Grayton would get the support of having me nearby.
+4	Less financial pressure and anxiety—might not have to work as much		
Total Weight: +19		Total Weight: −12	

Gloria concluded that the positive emotional benefits for her significantly outweighed the negative effects on others. She also realized that the biggest negative impact on others—kids losing their friends—would gradually improve as they adjusted to a new school and life in Grayton. Gloria's sense of guilt and wrongness significantly diminished when she completed this careful assessment.

Now it's time for you to do a needs assessment with a proposed solution/decision that apparently conflicts with the needs of others.

My Needs Assessment

The Problem:

Proposed Solution/Decision:

How the Solution Affects:

	My Emotional Needs		Emotional Needs of Others
Total Weight:		Total Weight:	

Using Coping Thoughts to Combat Guilt and Fear

Researcher Donald Meichenbaum discovered that we can inoculate ourselves against painful emotions with surprisingly simple coping thoughts (1977). These thoughts neutralize or replace the negative things we say to ourselves that generate guilt and fear. Here are some examples of coping statements that have helped people face unreasonable guilt about things they need to do to take care of themselves:

- I have the right to take care of myself at least some of the time.

- No one will take care of me except me.

- I've done a needs assessment and my decision is legitimate and reasonable.

- You can't make everyone happy all the time.

- It's okay sometimes to please yourself.

- _____ will be disappointed or even upset, but it will pass in time.

- I can't always meet _____ 's needs; there are times I have to balance things by looking after myself.

- Life is full of disappointments, _____ can cope and adjust to this decision.

- I can't afford *not* to take care of myself sometimes.

- I can't go on forever like I've been. I have to do something eventually even if _____ doesn't like it.

- I can be good to myself once in a while.

- _____ won't like it, but I need this for me.

- I have to keep a balance between doing things for me and doing things for others.

- I can be a good person *and* take care of myself once in a while.

- Taking care of yourself isn't selfishness—it's survival.

Coping statements can also help manage the anxiety that someone will be angry, or even reject you, if you put your own needs first. Here are some examples of coping statements that have helped people manage the fear of rejection—and do what they needed to do for themselves:

- Just because I'm anxious doesn't mean anything bad will happen. It's just a feeling I can cope with.

- They'll get over it. The upset will pass.

- They may be disappointed or angry, but we'll deal with it. We'll get through it.

- Time will heal this.

- It's an upset, people get upset all the time. They get over it.

- Nothing serious is going to happen.

- This anxiety won't hurt me—it just doesn't feel good.

- I can be anxious and still do what I need to do.

- I can cope with being anxious—I don't need to let it paralyze me.

- These are just scary thoughts, not reality.

- Upset and disappointment don't equal rejection. We'll get over this.

- I can cope with whatever happens.

- Fear won't defeat me. I can do this.

- Avoiding doesn't solve anything, I'm going to deal with this now.

- It'll be a hard conversation when I tell _____ about my plan. We'll get through it.

- I'll survive—however they react.

- It's not the end of the world if _____ gets mad at me. It'll blow over eventually.

- I have enough resources in my life to survive getting mad or upset. I don't like it, but I've got friends who'll still support me.

Example

Here's an example of how coping thoughts helped Richard, who wanted to stop going to church with his family. He disliked the pastor, the parishioners, and even the claustrophobic design of the church building. His wife, he knew, would be upset and castigate him for setting a bad example for their two sons.

Richard felt guilty that he was doing something that would hurt his wife, and perhaps even destabilize his family. His wife came from a very religious family, and he worried whether her need for a strong religious base might really alienate her when he stopped going to church.

To combat his guilt, Richard chose several coping thoughts that might give him courage when bringing the issue up with his wife. "I can't always meet Sheila's needs; there are times I have to balance things by looking after myself." And, "No one will take care of me except me." And, "Sheila will adjust; she'll just go to church without me."

Richard also chose several coping thoughts to manage his fear that Sheila would reject, or even leave him. "It's not the end of the world if Sheila gets mad at me. It'll blow over eventually." And, "Sheila's been angry at me lots of times before, and we've survived." And, "Time will heal this."

Richard wrote his coping thoughts down and read them over several times as he prepared to talk to his wife about the church issue. Sheila did, in fact, "blow a gasket" when Richard told her his decision. Things calmed down after a few days, and then there was another angry rebuke on the first Sunday he didn't go with the family to church. Three to four weeks after the announcement, things were mostly calm again. Sheila still thought Richard was setting a bad example for the kids, but she stopped complaining when he stayed home with the newspaper on Sunday.

Coping statements like those above can literally block out negative, "what if" thinking that focuses on all the bad ways someone else could react. Coping thoughts can calm you down and bring your attention back to the task at hand.

Some people find that the generic coping thoughts we've listed aren't quite suited for them. That's okay. You can write your own, or combine elements of the example coping thoughts into something that feels right to you.

In the space below, write four coping thoughts that might help you with the guilt that you've disappointed or hurt someone when you took care of yourself:

_____

_____

_____

_____

Now, in the space below, write four coping thoughts that might help you with the fear that someone will be angry, or even reject you:

_____

_____

_____

_____

Following Through

After you've completed your needs assessment, make a clear decision. Are you or aren't you going to take action in support of your own needs? Don't avoid, don't put it off. Avoidance is just decision by omission. If you decide that your needs significantly outweigh the negative consequences for others, set an actual date for implementation. Write it in your appointment book, and start preparing for it now. Develop coping thoughts that will help you with any guilt or anxiety, and use them when those feelings threaten to paralyze you. Remember, you have an *obligation* to take care of your mental health. Don't let the Core Belief of Primacy stand in the way of solutions and decisions that take care of you.

6

Testing Your Core Belief on Real Problem Solving

Right now we'd like you to choose a problem you would like to use this workbook to solve. It can regard any domain of your life. For the purposes of this exercise, it should be a problem where significant progress could be made in two to four weeks—if you took action. In other words, it shouldn't be a problem that requires you to go back to school, save to buy a house, or change your business from the ground up. The difficulties should be specific and discrete; action should somehow make things different. Just ahead, in the "Testing Your Core Beliefs Worksheet," you'll answer these two key questions for any core belief you choose to test:

1. What does your core belief about competence predict will happen when you attempt to solve this problem? How will things go wrong?

2. What compensating behaviors would you most likely resort to when trying to solve this problem?

These predictions, driven by your core belief, are very important. They're your failure nightmare. They make your attempt to change seem hopeless. And they discourage you from ever starting. At the bottom of the worksheet at the end of this chapter there's an empty box with the header, "What Really Happened." This is something you should fill in later, after you've worked the five problem-solving steps to change this problem. Obviously, we don't know what you're going to write in the box. But you may surprise yourself—the predictions driven by your core belief may not turn out to be accurate. You can repeat this same test every time you do some new problem solving—four worksheets are provided. Write down all the things your core belief tells you might go wrong; how you'll screw it all up. Then go back later and write down what really happened. Over time, this kind of testing can profoundly change how you see yourself.

Coping with the Fear of Failure (Without Compensating Behaviors)

Coping with any fear takes work. And planning. Even then, the fear won't go away—it will just be more manageable. Coping with the fear of failure requires four steps:

1. learning to relax in the face of the fear,

2. learning to replace "what if" thoughts with coping thoughts,

3. making a coping plan, and

4. making a commitment to cope rather than avoid.

Learning to Relax

When you feel anxious about your ability to do something, when thoughts of failure pressure you to avoid a challenge, physical relaxation can help. The quickest, and arguably the best, relaxation technique available is cue controlled relaxation (McKay et al. 1997). It's easy to learn, and the effects can be every bit as powerful as a dose of Xanax. Here's how you do it:

1. *Learn to take a deep, diaphragmatic breath.* To accomplish this, put one hand on your chest, and the other on your stomach—just above your belt line. Now take a deep breath that moves only the hand above your belt. Not the hand on your chest. Practice for a few minutes till you get it. The idea behind a diaphragmatic breath is that it pushes the air down toward your abdomen, stretching and relaxing your diaphragm. When your diaphragm relaxes, it sends a message to the emotion centers of your brain that all is well, no danger's imminent.

   If you have difficulty getting the hand on your belt line to move without moving your chest, try this. Press down with the hand on your belt, and then try to breathe so that you push the hand back out. Keep practicing at pushing that hand out until it feels pretty easy to do. Make sure your chest hand is hardly moving. Most of the air should be directed downward—pushing your stomach out.

   Practice diaphragmatic breathing just before each meal and prior to bedtime. Within a few days, it should start to feel easy and natural.

2. *Select a cue word.* This should be a word or phrase that symbolizes relaxation to you. It could be a peaceful color, the name of a place that relaxes you, or a simple command like "Relax now" or "Let go." Some people use spiritually centering words like "Om" or "One." It doesn't matter. Whichever word or phrase you choose will soon be linked in your mind to feelings of deep calm.

3. *Imagine a "moving band."* Imagine a band or a circle of light around your body. It starts just above your head, like a halo, then moves slowly downward to your feet. As it passes each region of your body—head, neck and shoulders, chest and back, stomach and arms, hips and hands, legs and feet—you feel a deep sense of relaxation begin in that area. Make a conscious effort to relax the muscles in each part of your body that the moving band passes.

   Go ahead and practice this for a few minutes. Visualize the circle of light moving gently down from your head to your feet, relaxing each muscle as it passes.

4. *Practice cue controlled breathing.* Now it's time to put these components together. You're going to take about ten diaphragmatic breaths. On each out-breath you'll say your cue word to yourself. As you breathe, visualize the moving circle of light relaxing each part of your body until you are totally, deeply relaxed.

This is going to take a little practice to get used to. Follow the same practice schedule you had for diaphragmatic breathing—before meals and bedtime. Do two complete sequences of ten breaths and the moving band each time you practice. Don't forget to always say the cue word to yourself on every out-breath. After a while, the cue word *alone* will trigger relaxation.

Once cue controlled breathing feels easy and natural, it's time to use it during times of stress. Anything that tenses or makes you anxious should be a signal to start cue controlled breathing. In particular, it will help when facing challenging problem-solving steps.

Using Coping Thoughts

When you're afraid of something, it's common to imagine catastrophes that make you even more fearful. Such negative thoughts eventually scare you into avoiding a challenge. And the decision to avoid suddenly makes you feel more relaxed. So scaring yourself is reinforcing because it makes you avoid, which makes you feel better.

This pattern is something you need to change. To overcome it you'll require a kind of psychological armor. Researcher Donald Meichenbaum discovered that we can inoculate ourselves against fear with surprisingly simple coping thoughts (1977). Here are some examples of coping statements that have helped people face their fear of failure:

- I can be anxious and still deal with this situation.

- This will pass—I can still do what I need to do.

- This is an opportunity for me to learn to cope with my fears.

- I'll ride this through—I don't need to let this get to me.

- I can take all the time I need to let go and relax.

- Whether I succeed or fail, I'll still survive, and I can deal with it.

- I can do what I need to do in spite of anxiety.

- I'll survive.

- This anxiety can't hurt me.

- Whatever happens, I can cope with it.

- If one thing doesn't work, I'll try something else.

- Things don't have to go perfectly, I can cope with mistakes.

- I'm trying, and that's what's important.

- Nothing serious is going to happen to me.

- These are just scary thoughts—not reality.

- I'll do my best, and accept whatever happens.

Coping statements like these can help you replace negative, "what if" thinking that paints pictures of all the ways you can fail. Coping thoughts literally block out the fear-inducing ones, and calm you down in the process.

Here's an example of how coping thoughts helped a young woman who needed to make a career change. Sandra was an order processor who was developing carpal tunnel symptoms. She needed a different kind of job, and worked the problem-solving steps to find an alternative. After a lot of brainstorming, she decided to take an editing class to see if she had any talent for copy editing. Almost as soon as she enrolled, the "what if" thoughts started: What if she was too "spacy" to edit? What if she couldn't understand the *Chicago Manual of Style*? What if she embarrassed herself in front of the class? What if she couldn't keep track of the minutia enough to be an editor? It went on and on.

To combat the anxiety triggered by this onslaught, Sandra chose a few key coping thoughts and repeated them to herself each time another "what if" came up. "I'm trying, that's all anyone can do," she'd say to herself. And, "Relax—whatever happens won't be the end of the world. I'll just try something else." And, "If I'm not cut out for editing, fine. I'm smart enough to do lots of things." And, finally, "Just do it."

Notice that Sandra didn't try to refute her negative thoughts. That road leads to a lot of crazy inner debate. Instead, she just affirmed that she could cope with whatever happened, and gave herself a boost for trying. The whole point of coping thoughts is to remind you that you have the strength and resiliency to face a challenge, and a setback isn't the horseman of the Apocalypse.

Some people find that the generic coping thoughts we've listed above aren't quite right for them. That's fine. Your task then is to write your own. Think of the problem-solving challenge you face. What could you say to yourself to make it less scary? For example, do you have skills that increase your chances for success? Or have you succeeded in a similar situation before? Do you have someone who will support and help you? Is there something you might enjoy about the challenge—no matter what happens?

Write a coping thought that offers comfort—either hope that you can succeed, or an affirmation that you can face the fear and the challenge, regardless of the outcome.

In the space below, write four of your own coping thoughts that might help with the fear of failure:

_____

_____

_____

_____

The Worst That Could Happen

One of the most effective ways to deal with fear is to ask this question: What's the worst thing that could happen? Depending on your problem-solving challenge, there could be a lot of answers: waste time, be very embarrassed, lose money, face anger or disapproval, be told "no," discover that you lack necessary abilities.

Sandra, just before her first editing class, tried this exercise. The worst thing that could happen, she wrote, was "having to quit in the middle because I couldn't keep up or I got feedback that I wasn't cutting it." How did she plan to cope?

- Tell the teacher before the first class that I don't want public feedback.

- I'll remind myself that it isn't the end of the world—I've only invested a few weeks in this.

- I'll start thinking about Plan B—getting an internship as an assistant publicist.

- I'll call my mother for a loan.

- I'll remind myself that editing is just one of a hundred career choices I could pursue.

Now think about your own fear of failure—particularly as it relates to possible solutions to a problem. What's the worst that could happen? Write it in the space below:

_____

Now let's explore what you'd do to cope if this worst case scenario occurred. Write down at least three things you could do to manage and get through such an event:

_____

_____

_____

Knowing how you'd cope can make a possible failure less scary. And give you more courage to face the challenge. However things turn out, you have in the back of your mind a few things you can do if the worst should happen.

How a Coping Plan Can Fight Fear

Making a coping plan is like building a sturdy platform that will always hold you up, no matter what. A good coping plan helps you control the fear of failure in three ways. First, you use relaxation skills to lower your anxiety—particularly when you're getting hit by a wave of fear that you won't succeed. Second, you choose three or four good coping statements to replace catastrophic, "what if" thoughts. Third, you plan an alternative behavioral response to replace avoidance. This might include things like

a. making an appointment with yourself to do the next step of problem solving,

b. calling someone for support,

c. promising yourself a specific reward for finishing the next step of problem solving,

d. taking a brief rest break, with a set time for returning to a problem-solving task,

e. turning off the TV, the computer game, and all other avoidance activities, and

f. going to a place where you can focus exclusively on a problem-solving task.

When the fear of failure strikes, and you start to feel like giving up or avoiding a new challenge, immediately put your coping plan into action.

Example

Sandra photocopied the coping plan and filled in her four coping statements, previously mentioned. Then she did a lot of thinking about her likely avoidance pattern with the editing classes. Sandra had responded to academic challenges in college by procrastinating till the last minute. Then she didn't have enough time to do a good job on the term paper or the final. Sandra often took Incompletes in these classes—and some of these had turned into F's.

Typical avoidance strategies included getting totally involved in an art project, nightclubbing with friends, planning elaborate birthdays for people, and getting swallowed by a good mystery novel. Whenever Sandra thought about her academic work, she'd lie to herself that she'd get to it the next weekend.

Here, then, is Sandra's list of coping behaviors to overcome fear-driven procrastination.

1. Set specific study times and never schedule something that conflicts.

2. Call Laura, who's promised to "make me study." She'll come over and get me focused.

3. Find a student whom I can call for an explanation if I get stuck, or e-mail the teacher.

4. Turn off all distractions—TV, radio, computer—and get busy right now.

5. Go immediately to the school library, and work in one of the little cubicles.

What helped Sandra most, it turned out, was being sure to do her coping behavior *on the same day* she felt anxious or noticed the impulse to avoid.

My Coping Plan

1. Do three minutes of cue controlled relaxation to physically calm yourself down.

2. As soon as your body is relaxed, review your coping thoughts. Write them here:

_____

_____

_____

Each time a negative, "what if" thought enters your mind, immediately replace it with a coping statement. Continue doing this till the anxiety abates.

3. The impulse to give up or avoid your problem-solving steps will be managed with at least one of the following four coping behaviors. Write them here:

_____

_____

_____

The coping behavior *must* occur on the same day that you felt the failure anxiety. Delay will reinforce avoidance.

Making a Commitment

Your coping plan will work, if you do it. And you'll successfully manage your fear of failure, if you follow your coping plan. Commit to yourself—and someone whose opinion matters to you—that you'll follow your coping plan for the next thirty days.

We call the person you commit to the "motivator." Explain to the motivator the problem-solving steps you've decided to take and your coping plan to keep on track if anxiety begins to affect you. Ask the motivator to check in with you at least once per week to monitor your progress.

Research shows that commitments to others are more effective than private decisions at changing behavior. Take advantage of this fact. Get the motivator involved, and talk to him or her often about your problem-solving efforts.

Testing Your Core Beliefs Worksheet

Core belief to be tested: _____

Problem you want solved: _____

Key Questions:

1. What does your core belief predict will happen when you attempt to solve this problem? How will things go wrong?

2. What compensating behaviors would you most likely resort to when trying to solve this problem?

Example

George was a police department property room clerk who was lonely and wanted to take someone to the annual PAL picnic instead of going alone as usual. He had his eye on a pretty patrol woman who had rotated into his precinct house, and another woman who worked in the building department down the street. Here's how he answered the key questions:

1. If I miraculously was able to ask either woman, they would treat me contemptuously, feeling insulted that a balding, overweight zero like me had the gall to ask them out.

2. I'd most likely wait until too it's late, go see one of them at the last possible moment, hem and haw like a total loser, end up asking some nerdy question about her job, and chicken out like the true coward that I am. Or I might not try at all, just have another donut and resign myself to loneliness.

George saw that his predictions and his compensating behavior were virtually guaranteeing that he would not ask anyone out, or if he did manage to ask the questions, guaranteeing that any woman would sense his self-doubt and turn him down.

The predictions you make from your core beliefs are very important. They are your nightmare scenario, the vision of disaster that keeps you from initiating change, and keeps you stuck.

Because George faced his prediction of failure and forewarned himself about his probable compensating behaviors, he was able to apply the problem-solving steps in the latter half of this book and become an active dater of women.

What Really Happened

Continue to test your core belief in this way. Pick a problem to solve, predict the likely outcome if you continue to be ruled by the debilitating core belief, alert yourself to your likely compensating behaviors, then solve the problem and compare what really happened to your initial prediction.

Part 2

Problem Solving

7

Assessment

The first step in any problem-solving process is assessment—clearly stating the problem itself. Many minor problems are solved with this step alone, often without even realizing that you are practicing problem solving. For instance, you start putting on your raincoat in a dark hallway and it feels funny. Without consciously thinking about it, you go through a lightning fast cycle of problem assessment and problem solution. If you could decipher the fragments of words and images that flash through your mind in the three seconds it takes you to straighten out your coat, it might sound like this:

Something's wrong . . . coat's funny . . . what's the problem here? . . . can't tell . . . take it off . . . the belt's tangled in the sleeve . . . straighten the belt . . . that's better . . . put it on and go.

This trivial scenario contains all the essential steps you will apply to one of your problems in this chapter: listing what's wrong, identifying a key problem, exploring all its aspects, and setting a goal for a solution.

Assessment in problem solving is like diagnosis in medicine. Just as a lasting cure is unlikely in medicine without an accurate diagnosis of the disease, so a lasting solution is unlikely in problem solving without a careful assessment of the problem. For example, the rash on your elbow may be poison ivy, psoriasis, allergy, or skin cancer. Until you know which one, you don't know which kind of remedy to seek. Likewise, your problem of feeling distanced and alienated from your brother may be due to a time conflict, residual sibling rivalry, preoccupation with his new child, or your own jealousy of his new wife. Until you know which, your attempts to solve the problem will not be focused and effective.

This chapter will help you pick a problem to start on, analyze it carefully, identify blocks to your search for a solution, and set a goal that specifies the kind of solution you seek.

Problem Checklist

The list that follows will help you begin to break your problems down into the general areas in which people typically have problems: feelings, relationships, work, finances, and so on.

Within each general area, consider each specific situation listed and check the box that best describes how much of a problem it is for you. Mark the appropriate box as follows.

None—No interference. This doesn't apply to me or doesn't bother me.

Little—This mildly affects my life and is a small drain on my energy.

Moderate—This has a significant impact on my life.

Great Deal—This greatly disrupts my daily existence and strongly affects my sense of well-being.

If you have trouble determining whether a situation is a significant problem for you, imagine that you are actually in the situation. Visualize the particular sights and sounds, people and places that you encounter in your life. Include the actions you and others take and the words you use. Make the situation as real for yourself as you can, then notice how upset you feel. Notice whether you feel angry, depressed, anxious, or confused. These are "red flag" emotions that indicate a problem area for you. The strength of your confusion or emotion will give you a clue to how significant the problem situation is to you, and which box you should check. If you experience problems that aren't listed, just fill them in under "other" in the appropriate category. Be sure you also rate their impact on your life.

My Problem Checklist

Emotions	None	Little	Moderate	Great Deal
Worrying				
Feeling angry a lot				
Feeling a sense of guilt				
Feeling very depressed				
Feeling shame				
Feeling nervous or anxious				
Phobias				
Lack of motivation				
Having a particular bad habit				
Religious problems				
Problems with authority				
Competing goals or demands				
Obsession with distant or unobtainable goals				
Feeling blocked from attaining goals				
Other _____				

Relationships

Not having many friends

Too little contact with the opposite sex

Feeling lonely

Feeling timid or shy

Not getting along with certain people

A failed or failing love affair

Feeling left out

Lack of love and affection

Vulnerability to criticism

Wanting more closeness to people

Not being understood by others

Emotions	None	Little	Moderate	Great Deal

Not really knowing how to converse

Not finding the right partner

Feeling rejected by family

Discord at home with partner

Not getting along with one or more of
the children

Feeling trapped in painful family situation

Insecurity, fear of losing partner

Inability to be open and honest with
family members

Desire for sex with someone other than partne

Conflict with parents

Having interests different from partner's

Interference by relatives

Marriage breaking up

Children having problems at school

Sick family member

Excessive quarreling at home

Anger, resentment toward partner

Irritation with habits of a family member

Worry about family member

Other _____

Work/Career

Monotonous and boring work

Poor relations with boss or supervisor

Feeling stressed and overworked

Wanting a different job or career

Needing more education or experience

Fear of losing job

Emotions   None   Little   Moderate   Great Deal

Not getting along with co-workers

Unemployment

Unpleasant working conditions

Needing more freedom at work

Other _____

Pleasure/Recreation

Not having enough fun

Ineptitude at sports or games

Too little leisure time

Wanting more chance to enjoy art
of self-expression

Little chance to enjoy nature

Wanting to travel

Needing a vacation

Inability to think of anything fun to do

Other _____

Financial

Difficulty making ends meet

Insufficient money for basic necessities

Increasing amounts of debt

Unexpected expenses

Too little money for hobbies and recreation

No steady source of income

Too many financial dependents

Other _____

Environment

Bad neighborhood

Too far from work or school

Too small

Emotions   None   Little   Moderate   Great Deal

Unpleasant conditions

Things in need of repair

Poor relationship with landlord

Other _____

Health/Energy Level

Tired, feeling run down all the time

Difficulty sleeping

Weight problems

Stomach trouble

Chronic physical problems

Difficulty getting up in the morning

Poor diet and nutrition

Disabled

Other _____

Intellectual

Needing or wanting more education

Lack basic knowledge in some areas

Lack of creative or intellectual stimulation

Other _____

Problem Analysis

Look over the Problem Checklist you have just completed and ask yourself, "Which general category causes the most problems in my life?" From that area, pick one of the situations that you have rated as interfering with your life moderately or a great deal.

Using the situation you have chosen, fill out the Problem Analysis Questionnaire that follows. Some of the questions will be more applicable to you than others, but try to put at least one word in each space. When a space is not large enough for your full answer, use a separate piece of paper.

It's important that you not skimp on this exercise. Your problem will become much clearer in your mind by your spelling out the specifics and listing previous obstacles to solutions.

Example

Kathy is a thirty-two-year-old customer service representative for a phone company. She often suffers from stomach troubles that a doctor in the past had dismissed as "gastritis." She tried antacids and various changes to her diet, but they didn't help much. Here is how Kathy analyzed her upset stomach problems.

Kathy's Problem Analysis Questionnaire

Situation (refer to the problem checklist or briefly describe in your own words)

Chronic stomach cramps, diarrhea, nausea.

Who else is involved and what is their relation to you?

Mom lives with me and cooks too much spicy food. Friend wants to go to Mexican restaurants all the time.

What happens? What do you do and what do others do?

I eat things I can't digest well, get sick and feel miserable. Others are annoyed—"It's all in your head. Live a little."

Where does it happen?

Parties, restaurants, at home when Mom cooks.

When does it happen? What time of day? How often? How long does it last?

Worse when I'm under stress. Worse late at night. Happens three to four times a week. Lasts all night.

How does it happen? What rules does it seem to follow? What moods are involved?

Some foods look and taste good so I overindulge, or I don't want to offend by turning something down. I feel guilty saying no.

Why does it happen? What reasons do you or others give for the problem?

I say I have a delicate stomach. Others say it's psychosomatic. Some say ulcers, others say allergies. I don't really know what foods cause the problem.

How do you feel? Angry? Depressed? Sad? Confused?

Depressed. Angry at myself when I overindulge. Resentful of Mom and others who don't seem to care that I feel rotten.

Blocks to Problem Solving

Which of the four common blocks did you experience?

Primacy of others' needs—the feeling that "I shouldn't":

I shouldn't refuse what others have taken the time and trouble to prepare.

Incompetence—the feeling that "I can't":

I'm too wishy washy to say no to problem foods. I'm too dumb to figure this out.

Unworthiness—the feeling that "I'm too ashamed, worthless":

Sometimes I feel damaged or mortally ill.

Vulnerability—the feeling that "I'm too scared":

I'm afraid to find out I've got stomach cancer or some other deadly problem.

When Kathy looked at her analysis, she realized that she had been minimizing and dancing around her problem, worrying about what others' thought of her, and avoiding her fear of a cancer diagnosis to really tackle the problem head-on. The analysis gave her some hints about goals for the future and possible solutions. Perhaps she should have committed to the food allergy regimen, recommended by her doctor, long enough to find out whether she was allergic to something common like milk or wheat gluten. Perhaps if she worked on her ability to say no, it would help her avoid problem foods.

My Problem Analysis Questionnaire

Situation (refer to your problem checklist or briefly describe in your own words):

_____

Who else is involved and what is their relation to you?

_____

What happens? What do you do and what do others do?

_____

Where does it happen?

_____

When does it happen? What time of day? How often? How long does it last?

_____

How does it happen? What rules does it seem to follow? What moods are involved?

_____

Why does it happen? What reasons do you or others give for the problem?

_____

How do you feel? Angry? Depressed? Sad? Confused?

_____

Blocks to Problem Solving

Which of the four common blocks did you experience?

Primacy of others' needs—the feeling that "I shouldn't":

_____

Incompetence—the feeling that "I can't":

_____

Unworthiness—the feeling that "I'm too ashamed, worthless":

_____

Vulnerability—the feeling that "I'm too scared":

_____

Setting Goals for Solutions

After you have analyzed your problem, you're ready to set goals for solutions. In the pages to follow, you will begin by listing the past solutions you've tried, examining your obstacles, and constructing your goals.

Example

Here is how Kathy evaluated her past solutions and came up with her statement of goals.

Kathy's Past Solutions		
What worked?	**What didn't work?**	**What was irrelevant?**
Turkey and rice allergy diet (until I got bored)	Arguing with people	Most attempts at being assertive made me so nervous I got stomach pains anyway.
Lowering stress level in general	Antacids	Macrobiotics, fad diets
	Trying to change Mom's recipes	Fasting
	Obsessing about it	

My Past Solutions

What worked?	What didn't work?	What was irrelevant?

Next, look at what worked for you in the past and review your analysis of the problem. Use all the information you have detailed about the problem to write a comprehensive goal. Your goals should describe what would represent a solution to you. It should include everything that would need to change about the problem situation for you to consider the problem solved.

Look over all the "who, what, when, where" information you have amassed about the problem and be as specific and detailed as necessary in your goals. Wherever possible, state your goals in terms of actions you could take, exact amounts or dates, and key events or accomplishments by which you can later measure your results. Consider carefully the blocks to problem solving as well, and include the overcoming of pertinent obstacles as part of your goal.

Example

When Kathy looked at what worked for her in the past, she saw that she had some results from approaching her problem as an allergy and from lowering her stress level in general. She noticed that hassling with other people about food was not productive—nor was her free-floating anxiety or her specific fear of stomach cancer.

When she reviewed her entire analysis and past solutions, she found these key questions particularly meaningful:

Key Questions to Guide You in Stating Your Goals

- Who do you want to be involved in the solution? *Just me—my Mom and friends are irrelevant.*

- What has to happen for the problem to be solved? *No physical symptoms.*

- What do you need to do? *Make checkup and allergist appointments.*

- What do others need to do? *Nothing.*

- What specific bad feelings will go away? *Anxiety, depression, anger.*

- What specific good feelings will result? *Comfort, confidence.*

- Can you put a dollar or size figure on the solution? *Need to feel physically good 90% of the time.*

- What partially successful solutions from the past will you include? *Allergy approach and stress reduction.*

- What bad or irrelevant solutions will you avoid? *Blaming and hassling with others.*

- Will you need to overcome feelings of incompetence—the feeling that you really can't solve this problem? *Yes—by getting expert diagnosis.*

- Will you need to overcome feelings of vulnerability—the feeling that it's too scary or risky to attempt a solution to this problem? *Yes—need to face fear and find out the truth.*

Answering these key questions helped Kathy state her goals in the form of four sentences, each beginning with "I will" to reinforce her resolve:

Kathy's Goals for Solutions

- I will be able to enjoy food without getting sick 90% of the time.

- I will stop being afraid of the unknown, especially cancer, so that I can focus on an effective solution for good health

- I will figure out the real cause of my stomach problems for once and for all—disease, allergy, stress, or some combination.

- I will be assertive about food only when really necessary to safeguard myself, otherwise no whining to others.

You can see that Kathy is well on her way to a solution. Carefully assessing her stomach problems and evaluating her past attempts to solve them has pointed the way to a likely solution. She will need to gather more information, in the form of medical diagnosis and advice. She will have to avoid her past tendencies to blame her mother and friends for her problem. She'll also be on guard against her own tendency to feel vulnerable and incompetent when she experiences setbacks. But the way to an effective solution is much clearer than before.

Key Questions to Guide You in Stating Your Goals

- Who do you want to be involved in the solution?

- What has to happen for the problem to be solved?

- What do you need to do?

- What do others need to do?

- When will the solution take place?

- How will it happen?

- What specific bad feelings will go away?

- What specific good feelings will result?

- Can you put a dollar or size figure on the solution?

- What partially successful solutions from the past will you include?

- What bad or irrelevant solutions will you avoid?

- Will you need to overcome feelings of subjugation—the feeling that others will be upset if you really try to solve this problem?

- Will you need to overcome feelings of incompetence—the feeling that you really can't solve this problem?

- Will you need to overcome feelings of unworthiness—the feeling that you don't really deserve to solve this problem?

- Will you need to overcome feelings of vulnerability—the feeling that it's too scary or risky to attempt a solution to this problem?

Finally, write your full statement of goals here. Revise and refine them so that it's as short and clear as possible, but complete and comprehensive as well. The more time and care you take with this goal statement, the easier you will find the next chapter on brainstorming to be.

However, many problems are more complex than Kathy's. They require more imagination or inspiration to solve. When you need to get "outside the box" of your past solutions entirely, you need to embark on the adventure called *brainstorming*, the subject of the next chapter.

My Goals for Solutions

8

Brainstorming

In the 1950s and early 1960s researcher Roger W. Sperry and teams of students at Cal Tech studied brain structure and function. By observing and testing seizure patients who had undergone radical brain surgery, Sperry and others mapped out the specialized functions of the left and right hemispheres of the brain.

They discovered essentially that, in 98 percent of humans, the left half of the brain specializes in tasks requiring logic, language, and a linear, step-by-step approach. The right half of the brain specializes in tasks requiring intuition, imagination, and a more free-form, creative approach. The logical left brain solves problems by proceeding from A to B to C to D. The intuitive right brain solves problems by skipping from A directly to D, or even M, X, or Z.

When you have a persistent problem that hasn't yielded to the more obvious solutions that have occurred to you, you need to quiet your normally strident left brain and give your right brain a chance to generate some more intuitive, novel ideas. The word for this process is *brainstorming*.

In 1963, Alex F. Osborn published the third edition of his *Applied Imagination: Principles and Procedures of Creative Problem Solving,* with a chapter on a topic he called "Brainstorming." Artists, educators, psychologists, business people, and even government bureaucrats picked up on his ideas and the term became a permanent part of the English language. Today, there are countless books, seminars, workshops, videos, Web sites, cassette tapes, even games and computer software designed to help you learn the skill of brainstorming.

The current buzzword for brainstorming is "box," as in "think outside the box." A whole literature and business consulting industry has grown up around these ideas. The "outside the box" phrase has become such a cliché that there is a whole series of Dilbert cartoons about it and a Richard Bolles' book called *The Three Boxes of Life: And How to Get Out of Them* (Ten Speed Press 1978).

Alex Osborn died in 1966, but his book is still in print. Although his rules of brainstorming have been paraphrased and elaborated a thousand times, they have never really been topped:

No criticism allowed

The crazier the better

The more the better

Combine and improve on ideas

Rules for Brainstorming

1. No Criticism
Your logical, linear left brain tends to be conservative and highly suspicious of anything novel or unconventional. It acts as a censor, passing judgment on all your ideas the moment they occur to you. Your left brain compares each new thought to a whole series of standards to make sure that every idea is logical, possible, rational, respectable, legal, affordable, moral, safe, dignified, expedient, profitable, politically correct, and so on.

In the face of this relentless scrutiny, most creative, innovative ideas wither and die before they are fully formed. At the first hint of novelty or imagination, your left brain tends to shy away, telling you, "That's weird . . . that's crazy . . . that will never work." That's why many people try the same unsuccessful solutions to their problems over and over. Even though the failed strategies of the past don't work, their familiarity guarantees that they are the only approaches that make it past the left brain censor to be put into practice.

Therefore, the first rule of brainstorming is "No criticism." In the brainstorming exercise that follows, and every time you brainstorm a new list of ideas, you must firmly tell yourself, "No criticism allowed. Anything goes." As soon as you find yourself criticizing your own ideas or thinking they are crazy or way off base, learn to muffle that carping, critical voice in your own head.

For example, if you are brainstorming ideas for how to get out of debt, include whatever far-fetched, unlikely, or desperate measure that pops into your mind: "Rob a bank; sell a kidney; knock off rich Uncle Hubert; start a pyramid scheme; torch the credit bureau; etc." Don't stifle the flow of ideas by trying to evaluate or edit them. Do whatever it takes to turn off your left brain critic for a while. Imagine that you have a *Get Out of Criticism Free* card that allows you to express any and all ideas that might bubble up from your more creative side. Promise your internal critic that you will criticize and analyze later.

2. The Crazier the Better

The best ideas often come out of left field, appearing completely nuts at first. This is one time when you don't want to be sane. Let yourself go. Deliberately look for the wackiest ideas you can concoct. Ask yourself how a total lunatic would solve this problem. Pretend that you are playing the part of a crazy inventor in a movie—whatever it takes to quiet your internal critic and access your more intuitive, inventive powers.

At this stage, if you think of something and the first thing that comes to your mind is, "That's crazy" or "that's stupid," congratulate yourself and underline that idea on your list. It's just what you want. For example, if you are brainstorming methods of getting your twenty-three-year-old son to move out of the house, you should welcome notions such as, "Put itching powder in the sheets; a trail of breadcrumbs out the driveway; make him sleep in the yard; nail the doors shut; paint all the windows black; start charging for air breathed." You wouldn't really do any of these things, but they will suggest possibilities that you might not think of otherwise.

If you have trouble coming up with crazy ideas, ask yourself what kind of solutions would be suggested by a genuinely crazy person, a complete lunatic who hears alien voices or thinks he's Saint John the Baptist. Likewise, how would your dog solve this problem? How would Dracula or Mickey Mouse solve it? There's a great old joke about a guy fixing a flat tire outside an insane asylum. All five lug nuts roll to the bottom of a long hill and he is about to hike down to retrieve them when an inmate suggests, "Why don't you use one nut from each good wheel to hold the spare tire on long enough to drive down the hill, rather than walking all that way?" The motorist exclaims, "How did you come up with such a clever idea?" And the inmate replies, "I may be crazy, but I'm not stupid."

Problems are no fun, but brainstorming can be. Allow yourself to cut loose and enjoy being a little off-the-wall silly. Humor is often a shortcut to creativity. It's more common than you'd think to find the germ of the final solution in an idea you first proposed as a joke.

3. The More the Better

Quantity counts more than anything in brainstorming. The more ideas you list at first, the more you have to combine and improve upon later. The *quality* of the ideas you refine at the end of the process depend directly on the *quantity* of ideas you generate at the front end.

Sometimes the true nature of a problem is not visible from a single point of view. Remember the fable about the blind seers who examined an elephant for the first time? Each one took hold of a different part of the beast and judged the whole by the part. The blind man at the tail said the elephant is "like a rope." The one at the side focused on the wall-like nature of the elephant, the trunk guy emphasized the snakelike nature of the elephant, and so on.

Brainstorming is a way of becoming your own committee of seers—multiplying and shifting your own point of view of your problem so that you can see its full extent and true nature. Sometimes you may find that you've been trying to solve a rope or wall problem that is actually an elephant problem. For this to work, you need a really large, divergent list of ideas.

In search of quantity, don't be afraid of repetition and similarity of ideas. For example, if you are trying to come up with ways of spending more time with your child away from the TV, go ahead and list all the minor variants that occur to you: "Read out loud with him; look at picture books together; look at magazines; cut out animals from magazines; color in magazines; color in coloring books; make collages; paste stuff in a scrapbook." All these activities involve printed materials, but they are subtly different. Listing them all keeps the ideas flowing and gives you lots of raw material for combining ideas later.

On the other hand, you may get stuck on a very repetitious train of thought that drowns out new ideas with an endless stream of essentially identical boxcars. If this is your tendency, allow yourself to follow one train of thought only for three or four items, then cut it off and clear the tracks for a new train.

4. Combine and Improve

When you have generated a long list of varied ideas, start combining and improving on the best ones. Now you can let out your mental clutch and re-engage your critical left brain. This is what your left brain is good at: noticing similarities and differences, making value judgments, and connecting the dots between steps.

Sometimes two or three mediocre ideas add up to one great idea. For example, the latch and the straight pin add up to the safety pin. The straight pin and the clothes pin add up to the paperclip. The clothes pin and the comb add up to the spring barrette.

Group similar ideas together and see if they add up to one superior idea. Compare wildly different ideas to see what makes them different. This is the time to notice that a beast like a rope, a beast like a snake, and a beast like a wall actually add up to an elephant.

Exercise — Brainstorming Session

Do this exercise when you are rested, alert, and have at least twenty minutes of privacy, safe from any possible interruptions. Unplug the phone, lock the door, turn off the TV and the computer, and give your problem the undivided attention it deserves. Using the same problem you worked on in Chapter 7 on "Assessment," pick one of your solution goals and write it at the top of the form that follows. Keep it short and suggestive, like these examples:

Spend more quality time at home

Get out of debt

Decide on a college

Stop worrying late at night

Avoid fighting with Joe

Note that these examples begin with an active verb. This is a good way not only to state your goal, but also to phrase the items on your brainstorming list. Use active verbs if you find it natural and easy, but don't let it slow you down. Some people brainstorm so quickly that they are lucky to write one legible word for each idea before going on to the next.

Sit comfortably and allow your mind to dwell on your problem and your desired goal for its solution. With a favorite pen or pencil, jot down whatever comes into your mind. Remember the first three rules for brainstorming:

No Criticism Allowed

The Crazier the Better

The More the Better

As long as the ideas keep coming, keep writing. Remember, quantity is everything. Don't stop until you have at least twenty items on your list. If you get stuck before twenty, put your pen down, stand up and jump around a little, then sit back down, take a deep breath, pick up the pen, and continue the list. This is like giving a balky appliance a little whack on the side to get it working again.

Example

Here is an example of a real brainstorming list. Carol was a single mom with twin boys age five. She took care of her kids during the day, then dropped them at her aunt's house at three o'clock and went to work at a hospital cafeteria until midnight. When her boys started school, she wanted to find a day job so she could be with them in the evenings and get to bed earlier. By late fall of their kindergarten year, she still had not found a new job. Nothing was available on the day shift at the hospital, and the day shift paid worse. She sat down one day and listed all her goals having to do with the job problem. Here is how she brainstormed ideas for her main goal:

Carol's Brainstorming List

Goal: Get a better-paying day job

Ideas:

1. Ask again at hospital personnel office

2. Ask about hospital jobs outside cafeteria

3. Look around town for good places to work

4. Ask at restaurants—be a waitress?

5. Take day job anyway in cafeteria and scrimp

6. Sell pencils on the street

7. Become a homeless beggar woman

8. Quit and live off credit cards

9. Try cafeteria at the college

10. Become a brain surgeon and make lots of money

11. Tell hospital personnel lady a sob story and try to get her interested in helping me.

12. Get Des Moines papers and look farther out from home

13. Go back to school and finish degree

14. Start a catering business of my own

15. Call up an employment agency

16. Ask Ruthie if she knows of any jobs

17. Make a resume

18. Buy a briefcase and a charcoal suit

19. Take work home

20. Sell my blood

21. Sell my body—no, that's night work

22. Sell the damn kids

Carol had trouble getting past twenty items. She got stuck after eight ideas and again at number eighteen. But she persisted until she had twenty-two, even though she thought she was getting silly and repetitious toward the end.

Combine and Improve

Save the last rule of brainstorming for last, when you have at least twenty items. Stop and go back over your list. Underline the most appealing ideas and ask yourself, "How can I improve on this?" Make revisions and write down any additional ideas you have. Use circles and arrows to combine several good ideas into one better idea. Rewrite the best ideas in a clear, forceful language. Revise using action verbs where appropriate.

Once Carol had enough ideas to work with, she went back over her list and combined and improved on it. She crossed out obvious bad ideas like living on credit cards, impractical options like becoming a surgeon, and frivolous notions such as dressing up like an executive. She combined several ideas about possible jobs at her current hospital. And she expanded and improved on ideas about other locations where she might work. Then she rewrote it like this:

Carol's Revised Brainstorming List

1. Hospital:

    a. Tell hospital personnel lady a sob story and try to get her interested in helping me.

    b. "I'll work days in any unit that pays same or better"

2. Other places:

    a. Make a list of all hospitals, schools, colleges, restaurants within ten miles

    b. Go through address book and call all friends and relatives, ask about jobs

    c. Make up a short resume

    d. Take it to a different place every day

3. Long term:

    a. Find out about junior college program for catering and hotel work

You may have to rewrite your list as Carol did, to make it clear which are the main ideas and which ideas go together. Carol found that the brainstorming session showed her that she had not really been looking for work effectively. She had been making assumptions about the unavailability of positions in her own hospital and ignoring other possible places to work in her own neighborhood.

My Brainstorming List

Goal: _____

Ideas:

1.

2.

3.

4.

5.

6.

7.

8.

9.

10.

11.

12.

13.

14.

15.

16.

17.

18.

19.

20.

Where to Go from Here

At the end of Chapter 7, you listed several goal statements, each representing an important part of your problem. For example, in addition to Carol's main goal of getting a better paying day job, she also had two other goals relating to her job and finance statements:

1. Make a longer term career plan

2. Start saving for a house down payment

Carol's brainstorming list of ideas for getting a better job included a couple of ideas about working in the catering field in the future, but her longer term career plans deserved a brainstorming session of their own. Likewise, she needed to brainstorm separately to come up with ideas for putting money aside for a down payment on a house.

Apply the brainstorming techniques you have learned in this chapter to each of your goal statements, so that you will generate ideas that cover all aspects of your problem. When you have combined and improved upon the best ideas from several brainstorming sessions, you'll be ready to consider the next chapter and the next step in problem solving: Consequences.

If you draw a complete blank when you sit down to brainstorm, try "seeding." When chemists are trying to make a saturated solution crystallize, they often have to drop a "seed" crystal into the test tube to get the reaction started. To crystallize ideas in your mind so that you can write them down on your brainstorming list, almost any seed can work. Open a dictionary at random and tell yourself that you are going to make up a possible solution using the first word that you see. For example, Charles was stuck coming up with ideas of what to do with his free time after retirement. He opened the dictionary three times at random. *Ride* gave him the idea of taking a ride on every road in his county. *Parachute* reminded him that he had always wanted to look up all his old army

Helpful Brainstorming Hints

Some people hate to write out lists in longhand. The ideas come too fast and writing slows them down. If this is your problem and you're a fast typist, do your brainstorming on your computer keyboard. Or you can talk into a tape recorder and transcribe your ideas on to paper later, when the spate of ideas has slowed to a trickle.

Other people are slow thinkers on their own, but they love to bounce ideas off other people. If that's you, try brainstorming in a group. When a few family members or friends are available, ask them: "Would you help me figure out what to do about _____?" As the leader of a group brainstorming session, you have five duties:

1. State the problem simply and clearly.

2. Explain and enforce the rules: no criticism, the more the better, the crazier the better, combine and improve at the end.

3. Write the list.

4. Keep people on the topic.

5. End the session, summarize the best ideas, thank the participants.

buddies on the Internet. *Ball* suggested taking in a game at the newly opened baseball stadium nearby.

Besides being the likely seat of your mind and soul, your brain is also a physical organ of your body. Your brain works better when it's rested, well-nourished with highly oxygenated blood, and undistracted with other tasks like worrying about the rent and listening for the phone. Do your brainstorming when you are mentally most alert. For most people, this is in the morning after a good night's sleep. Whether you're a morning or evening person, try this brain tune-up before brainstorming:

1. Get your heart rate up and your blood moving by jogging, walking, or dancing to music you like.

2. Lie down on your back with legs slightly apart, hands resting on your chest, and eyes closed.

3. Focus on your pounding heart and your breathing; take deep, full breaths as your heart and respiration rates slow down.

4. Empty your mind by counting your breaths or saying with each inhalation, "Breath arises," and with each exhalation, "Breath subsides."

5. Allow your problem to quietly enter your mind and notice what occurs to you.

More often than not, this exercise will focus and stimulate your brain to come up with more creative and perceptive ideas than you normally can invent with the tired, overworked, distracted, and starved brain that we carry around in our heads most of the day.

Sometimes you can enlist the power of suggestion and your subconscious mind in the brainstorming process. When you go to bed at night, tell yourself that a possible solution is going to come to you during the night. You may have a dream that suggests a novel solution, or you may come up with a good idea in the drowsy state just before you drop off to sleep or wake up fully in the morning. This happens regularly enough for a problem solving cliché like "sleep on it" to hold true.

If you're really stuck in a rut, you can try "paradoxical reframing." In this approach you put a whole new frame around the problem by taking the contrarian position that the problem represents the best of all possible worlds. For example, make a list of all the ways you could perpetuate and deepen the problem. Include on your list all the advantages of the problem, all the good things it brings to your life. Most of us are experts on making our problems worse, so this kind of paradoxical list is a great way to shed some light on the extent of the problem, what keeps it going, and just maybe how the process of problem perpetuation could be interrupted and stopped.

Other ways of reframing a problem are to recast it as another kind of problem. For example, it's not your personal problem, it's everybody else's public problem. Not a financial problem but a relationship problem. Not a scheduling problem but an assertiveness problem. Not job related but mood related, not scientific but emotional, not geographical but mathematical.

A final method of reframing is to abandon words for a while and try switching sensory modalities. You can use visual images or your senses of touch, taste, and so on to access your right brain more directly. For example, if you are stuck in your search for a partner, put the written goals and brainstorming lists aside. Forget about words and instead paint an abstract portrait of your loneliness. Then paint a portrait of your ideal partner. Let color, line, and form describe the problem and its solution. See if the purely visual mode gives you any inspiration before returning to your written lists.

You can also use your other senses such as taste or touch or hearing to illuminate your problem and inspire solutions. For example, if not having enough money left at the end of the month tastes like vinegar, feels like cold tin, and sounds like whistling wind, what would enough money feel, taste, and sound like? Honey, warm socks, and violins? Wine, satin, and saxophones? The answers to these kinds of reframing questions are mysterious and personal. Only you know your answers and what they reveal about your problems and your solutions.

As you gain familiarity with brainstorming, you will probably begin to do it mentally. As soon as a problem enters your mind, you might start spinning off a list of possible solutions, mentally noting the good ideas. This is fine for casual problems that come up in the course of daily life. But for serious, persistent problems, nothing beats the paper and pencil list. There are several advantages in putting your ideas down on paper: it helps you remember every item, underscores the importance of the problem in your life, focuses you on the search for a solution rather than just worrying about the problem, and gives you a little distance from your solution ideas so that you can more objectively evaluate them.

9

Consequences

As your experience in the last chapter on brainstorming taught you, not all ideas are created equal. Even among good ideas, some ideas are better than others.

In this chapter you will learn a systematic, objective way to evaluate the likely consequences of putting your various good ideas into practice. You'll identify the very best idea that you should try first—the one with the most positive consequences and the fewest negative consequences.

The heart of this chapter is the Consequences Chart, which you will become an expert at filling out. To get the most out of the chart, you will need to understand the key terms: strategy, consequences, and impact.

Strategy

In the last two chapters on assessment and brainstorming you were encouraged to use action verbs in describing your problems and ideas for solving them. That's because very few problems are solved by doing nothing or adopting a vague change in attitude.

The Consequences Chart asks you to describe three "strategies" for solving a problem. You often hear this word in reference to election campaign tactics. Considering the consequences of your possible actions is very much like planning a campaign: "I'll hit him with this, then he'll probably defend himself by doing this, which means I'll have to regroup and do that, and he'll counterattack with the other thing—"

Strategizing isn't limited to conflict situations—it can be used in every area of your life. If you are trying to make peace in your family, for example, you are looking for a strategy—a list of things you can do that will have the desired result of Dad talking to Mom again, sister coming to the wedding, brother cooperating with the trustee of the estate, and so on.

The key to a good strategy statement is to use action words that describe specific actions you might take, spelling out what, when, where, and how. Avoid vague expressions and open ended statements of intention. Here are several poor strategy statements and better revisions:

Poor	**Better**
Be more considerate	Ask Joan about her feelings daily
Get on the fast track	Write memo applying for supervisor position
Watch less TV	Put TV in closet
Get more exercise	Enroll in Beth's 7 A.M. yoga class
Improve qualifications	Take state certification exam next August

Consequences

Sir Isaac Newton said that for every action there is an equal and opposite reaction. You don't have to be a physicist or any other kind of scientist to know that this is the way the universe works, in a series of actions and reactions, causes and effects. In everyday human affairs, nothing happens in a vacuum. Every action you take has some kind of reaction from others. Everything you do is a cause that will have an effect.

This is what we mean by consequences: the likely reactions to your strategies for change. Consequences can take the form of actions by others or changes within yourself. For example, a declaration of love for your girlfriend might have positive or negative consequences. She might say, "I love you too," and you might experience a warm feeling of security and well-being.

Likewise, instead of saying, "I love you too," your girlfriend might say, "Then why did you sleep with Sally?" And you'd feel guilty and defensive instead of warm and cuddly. When you fill out the Consequences Chart, give equal time to the positive and negative possibilities.

Most strategies will have both positive and negative consequences, since few important decisions are all good or all bad. Everything important in life has an upside and a downside. If you and your girlfriend pledge your mutual love, that's good. But it may also mean that you should stop fooling around with Sally, and that's bad. This dualistic nature of human decision making is the fountainhead from which all those good news/ bad news jokes flow.

Impact

When you are considering the likely consequences of your strategies, it isn't enough to just divide them into positive and negative. You have to assess their overall impact on your life. The Consequences Chart asks you to rate the impact of each consequence on a scale from one to ten, with one being a very minor impact and ten being a very major impact.

To rate impact, you need to ask yourself whether the good consequences are really wonderful or just convenient. Are the bad consequences really horrible or just inconvenient? Do the consequences affect you directly or indirectly? Are they long-term or short-term consequences? Do they affect primarily you yourself or other people?

For example, if you quit your minimum wage job, move back in with your parents, and go back to junior college to get a software certification, what are the consequences? On the positive side, you don't have to work a boring job, you get to study something interesting, and you can get a better job later. The first two are short-term conveniences, the latter is more long term and important to your career. All three relate to you alone. On the negative side, you'll have to live with your parents, you'll have no money, and it's a big imposition because your dad wants to turn your old room into a home office. These are all short-term disadvantages—the first two affecting you and the latter affecting your parents.

Here are the guidelines for weighing the impact of different consequences:

Major outweighs minor

Long-term outweighs short-term

Direct outweighs indirect

Self outweighs others

This last guideline listed above is the most relative. It means that consequences affecting you personally are of greater importance than consequences affecting others—all else being equal. This is not an excuse to ride roughshod over the rights of other people. Whether your personal consequences outweigh those affecting others is a difficult judgment to make—it depends on which consequences and which other people are involved. Certainly you are justified in taking a course of action that results in significant, direct, long-term benefits to you and only minor, short-term, indirect disadvantages to others.

On the other hand, a solution that seriously harms others while providing you with a few minor, short-term advantages is no solution at all. To take an extreme example, pocketing $150 that you were supposed to turn in to the Community Chest is a poor solution. Even if you don't get caught, the temporary solution to your cash flow problem is outweighed by the damage you do to the other people who were supposed to get the money. Also, if you add your guilt, anxiety, and lowered self-esteem to the equation, the cash flow advantages really appear lightweight, and you begin to realize that the negative consequences affect you as well as faceless others.

Consequences Chart Directions

From your best brainstorming ideas developed in the last chapter, pick the three strategies that seem strongest and compare them using the three-page chart that follows. It's important to evaluate more than one strategy at a time so you can compare their total impact and come up with the best plan of action.

If you have trouble identifying clear actions to evaluate, you might need to return to the brainstorming chapter. You might need to combine your ideas or recast them in the form of action steps so that you come up with concrete strategies to evaluate.

When you have three clear cut strategies listed on the chart, briefly describe the positive and negative consequences of each. Close your eyes for a moment and really imagine acting on your strategy. Visualize how it will affect you and others—emotionally, socially, financially, physically, and so on. Write each consequence down in a short phrase, in the positive or the negative columns.

When you can't think of any more consequences, give each consequence an "Impact Score" from 1–10, according to how serious its impact on your life will be. If a consequence is not a very big deal, affecting you or someone else slightly for a short time, give it a one. If it will be a little scary or tiring or disruptive to your routine or relationships for a while, give it a four or five. If a consequence will make a major change in your life for years to come, give it a nine or ten.

Total the scores for the positive and negative consequences. The winning strategy—the one you should try first—is the one whose positive consequences outweigh the negative consequences by the biggest margin.

Example

Here is an example of how Rowena filled out her Consequences Charts. Her problem was what to do about her widowed, aging mother who had broken her arm in a traffic accident, had become too forgetful to pay bills on time, was in danger of losing her home for non-payment of the mortgage, and was losing weight because she had stopped cooking for herself.

Rowena's Consequences Charts

Strategy 1: *Do for mom myself—drive her around, take food, pay bills with her monthly, clean her house.*

Positive Consequences	Impact 1–10	Negative Consequences	Impact 1–10
Emotional			
Feel like a good daughter	8		
Relationship			
Maybe get closer to her	4	*Probably fight more*	8
Work/Career		*Have to take lots of time off work*	7
Pleasure/Recreation		*Less time for myself*	7
Financial			
Cheapest solution	7		
Environment		*She's still unsafe when I'm not there. She'll break her promise and drive her car, maybe kill someone*	6
Health/Energy Level		*I'll be exhausted*	5
total:	22		36

Strategy 2: *Get her help—taxi company on speed dial, Social Security and bills on direct deposit and automatic payment, meals-on-wheels, housekeeper, part-time attendant, home nurse visits.*

Positive Consequences	Impact 1–10	Negative Consequences	Impact 1–10
Emotional			
Feel like a pretty good daughter	6	*She's shy with strangers*	3
More peace of mind	6		
Relationship			
She will appreciate the help	7	*There will still be conflict*	4
Work/Career		*Have to take some time off*	4
Pleasure/Recreation		*Less time for myself*	4
Financial		*Way more expensive*	6

Environment		She'll still be unsafe	4
		She could still drive	5
Health/Energy Level			
Less drain on my energy	8	*I'll still worry and fret*	4
	total: 27		34

Strategy 3. *Convince her to sell house and car; move into retirement community with Aunt Maisie.*

Positive Consequences	Impact 1–10	Negative Consequences	Impact 1–10
Emotional			
Peace of mind	10	*She hates change*	8
Relationship		*She'll resent me*	6
Work/Career			
Will probably save my job	6		
Pleasure/Recreation			
More time for me	5		
Financial			
Cheapest long-term	7	*Most expensive short-term*	5
Environment			
She'll be safe and cared for	9	*No access to car*	3
Health/Energy Level			
Least effort long-term	5	*Most effort short-term*	3
	total: 44		22

In Rowena's charts, notice how some strategies have simultaneous positive and negative consequences in the same category. For example, moving her mother into a retirement community would have a positive emotional consequence of giving her peace of mind, while at the same time having the negative emotional consequence of confronting her mother with unwelcome change. Financially speaking, the move would have a short-term negative consequence, but a long term positive consequence. The Consequences Chart is a good way to lay out and assess the impact of these kinds of direct/indirect and short-term/long-term outcomes.

Rowena was able to see that the only strategy that had a balance of positive consequences was to get her mother into Aunt Maisie's retirement community. It was the most difficult solution in terms of immediate expense and strain on her relationship with her mother, but over the long term it represented the only way to make sure her mother was safe and cared for.

Example

Here is another example of how Jocelyn filled out her Consequences Chart. Jocelyn was a thirty-two-year-old singer and fiddle player who clerked in a hardware store to make ends meet. She had moved out to the West Coast from her home town and family roots in the east, felt lonely, and moved in with Frank, the first man who paid her any attention. Now, two years down the road, she was tired of his moodiness, hot temper, and the way he alternated between ignoring her and belittling her. She had just met Billy, a sweet mandolin player, who was young and eager to "rescue" her into his rented house with two other musician roommates. Jocelyn used the Consequences Chart to pick the best strategy to solve her joint problems of loneliness and where to live.

Jocelyn's Consequences Chart

Strategy 1: *Stay with Frank and work on the relationship.*

Positive Consequences	Impact 1–10	Negative Consequences	Impact 1–10
Emotional *Avoid pain of break up*	4		
Relationship *Might bring us closer*	4	*Probably won't work*	8
Work/Career			
Pleasure/Recreation		*Boring*	3
Financial *Cheapest option*	6		
Environment *Nicer house*	2		
Health/Energy Level		*Tired of Frank, depressed*	4
Education/Knowledge			
total:	*16*		*15*

Strategy 2: *Move into Billy's house.*

Positive Consequences	Impact 1–10	Negative Consequences	Impact 1–10
Emotional *Exciting new love*	8	*Painful break up with Frank*	6

Relationship			
Exciting new love	6	*He's too young*	4
Work/Career			
Might get gigs with Billy's band	3		
Pleasure/Recreation			
Lots of music at Billy's house	5		
Financial		*More expensive*	7
Environment		*Messy house, small room*	6
Health/Energy Level			
Less depressed	4		
Education/Knowledge			
Could learn mandolin	1		
total:	27		23

Strategy 3: *Get my own apartment and learn to live alone.*

Positive Consequences	Impact 1–10	Negative Consequences	Impact 1–10
Emotional			
Maybe more self-esteem	8	*Definitely more loneliness*	10
Relationship			
Just date Billy	5		
Work/Career			
Pleasure/Recreation			
Would have time to study cello	3		
Financial		*Very expensive*	9
Environment			
Cleaner and neater	7	*Very small*	8
Health/Energy Level			
Might blossom	5	*Might wilt*	6
Education/Knowledge			
Learn to manage on my own	2		
total:	30		33

In Jocelyn's charts the winning strategy is number two, leaving Frank and moving into Billy's house, since the positive consequences outweigh the negative consequences by four points.

The absolute size of the total scores is interesting in Jocelyn's case. For the first strategy (staying with Frank) total scores are both relatively low, 16 to 15. This is typical of a low-risk, low-gain strategy: if it works out, things will be slightly better and if it doesn't work, things will be slightly worse. For the third strategy (striking out on her own) total scores are relatively high, 30 to 33. This is typical of a high-risk, high-gain strategy: if it works out, things will be terrific and if it doesn't work, things will be awful.

How did Jocelyn choose? She moved in with Billy. A year later she moved out to her own place. It was awful at first and terrific eventually.

My Consequences Chart

Strategy 1: _____

Positive Consequences	Impact 1–10	Negative Consequences	Impact 1–10
Emotional			
Relationship			
Work/Career			
Pleasure/Recreation			
Financial			
Environment			
Health/Energy Level			
Education/Knowledge			
total:			

Strategy 2: _____

Positive Consequences	**Impact 1–10**	**Negative Consequences**	**Impact 1–10**
Emotional			
Relationship			
Work/Career			
Pleasure/Recreation			
Financial			
Environment			
Health/Energy Level			
Education/Knowledge			
total:			

Strategy 3: _____

Positive Consequences	Impact 1–10	Negative Consequences	Impact 1–10
Emotional			
Relationship			
Work/Career			
Pleasure/Recreation			
Financial			
Environment			
Health/Energy Level			
Education/Knowledge			
total:			

In the next chapter you will learn how to make a "Do List" to turn your winning strategy into a manageable series of steps.

How to Be Objective

As you fill out your Consequences Charts you may find yourself "cheating"—weighting the impact scores to favor the strategies you hope will win. There are two ways to think about this. One way is to be thankful. You can consider your leaning toward a particular strategy as a sign that you intuitively know what course is right for you, and just go on to the next chapter and make a Do List to pursue that strategy.

However, if you suspect that you are being subjective out of fear or doubt or one of the other blocks to problem solving covered in the first half of this book, you need to force yourself to be more objective.

There are things you can do to enforce objectivity:

- Have a friend help you assign the impact scores.

- Imagine that you are your own therapist, consultant, executive coach, teacher, lawyer, or loving parent and assign the impact scores from that third-party point of view.

- Imagine that you are the hero of a novel or movie who is filling out the chart, and make the scene as realistic and believable as you can.

10

Do List

In this chapter you will learn how to break your best strategy down into a logical list of steps to do—a Do List. Many of the techniques in this chapter were pioneered not by psychologists but by business people concerned with decision making, time management, and goal setting. In many ways, your Do List is like a business plan or production schedule: a list of what you have to do, and in what order, to accomplish your goal. The only difference is that your goal is solving a personal problem rather than unloading a million Czech light bulbs or landing a juicy janitorial service contract.

To be effective, a Do List should be:

1. Action Oriented

Write your Do List with action verbs that describe specific activities, behaviors, and concrete accomplishments. This is the clearest, least ambiguous way to state a goal, and a subtle spur to action. Here are some examples of poor and better items:

Poor	Better
Better relationship with Marge	Apologize to Marge
Closets	Clean out closets
More positive attitude about self	Recite affirmations

2. Detailed

The more details you spell out, the easier it is to remember what you need to do and to know when you have really accomplished it. Here are some continuing examples:

Better	Best
Apologize to Marge	Call Marge and say, "I'm sorry, it was my fault"
Clean out closets	Empty closets, sort into save, trash, and give away
Recite affirmations	Recite two affirmations out loud every two hours

3. Timely and Logical

Put first things first. A good Do List proceeds through time logically from beginning to middle to end. If you want to make a jelly sandwich, you have to get the bread out of the bread box before you can spread the jelly and you have to spread the jelly before you eat the sandwich. If you are building a house, you logically must pour the foundation before you raise the walls, and raise the walls before you frame the house.

4. Incremental

By incremental we mean that the steps should start with the simpler, more basic, easier tasks and proceed to the more complex, advanced and difficult tasks. For example, if you need to write a major term paper or dissertation, you might start with buying index cards and pens, scheduling a trip to the library, and doing some background reading. This would prepare, inform, and train you for the middle steps of taking notes and outlining a table of contents. The middle steps will prepare you for the later steps of writing a first draft and revising it. If you made "Write first draft" your first step, it would be too enormous. You need to sneak up on big steps by manageable increments.

Instructions

Step 1. List Every Step

List everything you will have to do, as it occurs to you, in any order. To help you get started, imagine that it is some time in the future, a time when you have successfully solved your problem. Actually close your eyes, relax, and imagine that glorious day. From this future vantage point, look backwards and see yourself doing everything necessary to arrive at the solution. As steps occur to you, open your eyes, and write them down. Then close them again and keep imagining.

When Betty Lou tried this, she imagined that she was teaching English as a second language at the junior college, having successfully obtained her teaching credential and ESL certification. Working backward from that future time, she "remembered" all these steps along the way to her goal:

Got hired at junior college

Interviewed with department chair

Applied for the job

Graduated

Took education courses

Worked part-time

Lived with mom and dad

Gave up apartment

Took Spanish courses

Was accepted to returning student credential program

Saved enough money

Applied to credential program

Filled out application

Got application

Broke up with Jim once and for all

Got roommate

Got old transcripts

Talked to registrar about requirements

Quit full-time job

Step 2. Rewrite Steps in Time Sequence

Get a fresh piece of paper and rewrite your list in strict time sequence: first thing first, second thing second, third thing third. When you find a step that seems too big to accomplish all at once, break it down into two or three smaller, more manageable steps. For example, Betty Lou realized that she couldn't just move back into her parent's house in one fell swoop. She broke it down into:

Get parents to agree

Cut down on personal belongings

Move in

Even these three steps were pretty overwhelming, so she made some further subdivisions:

Get parents to agree:

> *Go to coffee with mom and talk it over*

> *See Dad after church on Sunday, offer to clean baths and do laundry in lieu of rent*

> *Set a time table for moving in and a deadline for moving out*

Cut down on personal belongings:

> *Get Jim to clean his junk out*

Have a garage sale

Sell old books to used bookstore

Give jewelry tools and bench to Judy on long-term loan

Move in:

Set move in weekend well in advance

Borrow Anderson's truck

Ask Judy and Delores to help

Step 3. Put Easy or Non-Time-Sensitive Tasks First

As you work out the time sequences, you'll find some actions that don't need to be done in a particular sequence. In that case, put the easiest, simplest, cheapest, smallest items first. In fact, look for some small, easy steps that you can put first, even if they could wait till later. This principle helped Betty Lou get started. She cleaned out her desk to have a clear place to work on her application, even though it was not due for several weeks. She wrote for transcripts and sold some old books early on as well, just because they were simple, easy tasks that would get her moving in the direction of her long-term solution. With a little momentum built up, she was able to tackle some of the more daunting steps.

Step 4. Use Multiple Columns for Parallel Tasks

If your strategy consists of several tasks that can be accomplished simultaneously, set up your time line with a separate column for each parallel task. Here is how Betty Lou arranged part of her time line that consisted of parallel tasks:

Write for transcripts	*Break up with Jim once and for all*
Pick up school application	*Get Jim's junk moved out*
Fill out application	*Advertise for roommate*

Step 5. Evaluate Consequences in "Either/Or" Situations

Sometimes there is more than one path to your goal and you can't decide which to pick. In that case, return to Chapter 9 on evaluating consequence and weigh the options using the guidelines there. Betty Lou's plan included two ways to save money on housing: clear out her ex-boyfriend's junk to make room for a roommate, or move back in with her parents later. At first she thought that she would keep her apartment and get a roommate, until school actually started, then she'd move in with her parents. When she weighed the consequences of each path, she realized that her parents were the better deal all around, and planned to move in with them earlier—skipping the roommate phase entirely.

Step 6. Add Dates

When you have all your steps in order, mark the first step "today." Mark the last step with the date by which you want to have it accomplished. Then mark all the intervening steps with "tomorrow, next week, in two weeks, by next month, in three months" and so on until you come out at the target date for completion. Use exact dates for deadlines when you can. You may have to juggle deadlines extensively to make the final date, or have to extend the final date to more realistically allow sufficient time for all the intervening steps.

Example

Here is Betty Lou's final Do List, dates and all.

Betty Lou's Do List

Today:

Send for transcripts	*Sell books*

Tomorrow:

Break up with Jim	*Talk to mom and dad*

Next Week:

Talk to registrar	*Place ad for garage sale*
Get application	*Get Jim's junk out*

Ask Prof Jens for letter of recommendation

By end of month:

Fill out application	*Give Judy jewelry stuff*
Ask about part-time job	*Have garage sale last weekend of month*
Check in with mom	

July 1st

Accepted into program	*Find part-time job*
Clean up old room	*Register for Spanish and Education classes*
Line up truck and help	

August 30

School starts	*Quit full-time job*
Start part-time job	

March Next Year

Apply for ESL job at JC

June Next Year

Graduate

July Next Year

Start teaching	*Apartment hunting*

Notice that as she approached the end of her time line, Betty Lou became less detailed. That's normal. No long-term strategy can be planned out day by day for months to come. You will have to revisit your Do List from time to time as you make progress, breaking the later steps down into more detailed lists of what to do tomorrow, next week, and so on.

Step 7. Do the Do List

The most beautifully and lovingly constructed Do List in the world is useless if you don't actually perform step one, then step two, and so on. Make sure you have the time, energy, money, and other resources to actually accomplish all these carefully sequenced steps, and do them. Pin your Do List up where you will see it often. Carry the detailed steps for today, tomorrow, and next month with you at all times. The next section suggests an effective way to do this.

Helpful Tools

A good tool for managing your Do List on a daily basis is the "T-schedule," a format for writing down what you have to do each day. You can go to an office supply store and buy a personal calendar and planner booklet laid out in T-schedule format, or you can make your own. The following will give you an idea of the basic layout:

My Daily Planner

Date: _____

Appointments	Tasks
8 A.M.	
9	
10	
11	
12 P.M.	
1	
2	
3	
4	
5	
6	
7–9	

Notes:

Buy a daily planner that is set up this way, or make your own in a small notebook. Have one of these layouts for each day of the next year, with the time divisions that make sense for your lifestyle. Write down anything that you have to do at a particular time—meetings, classes, doctor's appointments, lessons, interviews, and so on—under the appropriate day and time. That way you can tell at a glance where you have to be and what you have to do at any given hour of the day. Conflicts will be apparent and can be rescheduled before they turn into disasters.

In the right column, write down all the tasks you want to accomplish that day that do not have to be done at a particular time: writing letters, shopping, errands, studying, and so on. These tasks you will perform your free time when you don't have a meeting or an appointment. You may want to put some important, time-sensitive items in the left column, so that you know exactly when you plan to do them.

Keep your planner with you at all times. Whenever you make an appointment or remember something you want to do, jot it down on the appropriate day, under an exact time on the left or as a task on the right.

Each morning, get out your list and *before you do anything*, mark each non-time-sensitive task on the right with an A, B, or C. "A" tasks are top priority, things that absolutely have to get done that day. "B" tasks are important items that it would be nice to do today, but they could be put off until another day. "C" tasks are low priority items that can be put off several days without causing any trouble.

If it looks like a busy day, go one step further in your prioritizing and number all the "A" tasks in order of their importance. Then start over at one and number all the "B" tasks. The idea is that you will do A1, then A2, then A3 and so on, until all the As are checked off. Then you will start at B1, B2, and so on, then get to the Cs. This way, however far you get down your list, you will have spent the most time on the most important items.

Example

Here is a sample page from Betty Lou's daily planner:

Betty Lou's Daily Planner	

Date: *Thursday, March 14*

Appointments	Tasks
8 A.M.	(Day off work) A1 Copy Jen's letter ✓
9	Coffee with mom B1 envelopes ✓ When to paint room?
10	B2 Call newspaper w/ ad ✓
11	A3 Safeway—milk, bread, hose, ketchup ✓
12 P.M.	Lunch with Judy B3 Sort taxes *3-18 8 P.M.* garage sale and jewelry plans
1	C1 Call Bill J. **X**
2	
3	A2 Mail application—last P.O. pickup at 4:30 P.M. ✓
4	
5	
6	
7–9	

Notes:

Returning student financial aid—Madeline Grimmer, Eaton Hall, ext. 1123

Rent *Memento* video

Get *After the Breakup* (Watrous and Honeychurch 1999) at library

In the example above, Betty Lou gave highest priority to mailing her school application, since it had to be postmarked that day. Shopping for groceries, calling Bill, and sorting her taxes were lower priority and could wait if they had to.

Check off each item on your daily list as you deal with it. Use meaningful marks such as these:

✓   Done

—   Rescheduled

X   Canceled

If you decide to reschedule a task, page forward in your planner and write it down on the day you plan to do it. If you accomplish a task such as picking up an application, note the date the application is due and record that in your planner on or *before* the appropriate day. In the above example, you can see that Betty Lou put off sorting the taxes and crossed off calling Bill, since the question she had to ask him was answered by Judy at lunch.

Resist mightily the temptation to skip the boring or painful "A" items such as making dental appointments in favor of doing more pleasant "B" or "C" items like shopping for a new blouse. Don't clutter your daily list with things that you always manage to do anyway, like eating, watching favorite programs, or calling your best friend. Use your daily list for the important, time-sensitive jobs that you would otherwise forget, put off, or skip.

Use the "Notes" section to record information that you run across each day: the phone number of a new acquaintance, the title of a video you want to rent, the name of an organization you want to join, and so on. In the Betty Lou example, she noted a contact at the university, a video she wanted to rent, and the title of a self-help book that was recommended to her.

Consult your list often during the day, checking off tasks as they are accomplished and seeing what comes next. Review the list at the end of the day and take a moment to perform Do List housekeeping. Move unfinished items on to tomorrow or the next day. As you keep postponing certain kinds of tasks, you learn what is most difficult for you to accomplish. Some "C" tasks you can just cross out because they aren't important enough to ever do. Some "B" items, like making that dental appointment, might become "A1" if you get a toothache.

Transfer notes to files or address books or turn them into future tasks in your planner. Betty Lou transferred her note about financial aid to next Tuesday, when she planned to be on campus in order to stop by Eaton Hall and pick up an information packet from Mrs. Grimmer.

From time to time, get out your master Do List, update it, revise dates and tasks, and break later big steps down into more detailed small steps, then enter them in your daily planner for next week or next month. Betty Lou's Do List gave her detailed steps for applying to school, reducing her personal belongings, and moving back into her parent's house. When she started school, she had to dig out her Do List and generate some detailed schedules for getting to class, studying, writing papers, cleaning her mom's house, and so on.

This might seem like overkill. You may feel like you are pretending to be some kind of high-powered executive or becoming a slave to an arbitrary list format. It's true that many of these techniques have been perfected over the years by business people, but don't let that put you off. Some kind of daily discipline is required. Employ the tools that professionals have honed and perfected and use them for your own personal goal of solving problems and making changes in your life.

Personal Support Agreement

You can increase your chances of sticking to your Do List by soliciting support from a close friend or family member. Share your Do List with someone you respect and trust. Ask them to check in with you from time to time to see that you are still on track. Betty Lou asked her mother and her friend Judy to make her aware whenever they noticed that she was succumbing to inertia and procrastination.

Special Considerations

When you consistently fail to perform a step in your Do List, you are probably up against one of these three common problems:

1. Step Too Big

You aren't Superman. You can't leap tall buildings in a single bound. But you can break giant steps down into a series of manageable baby steps: go into the tall building's lobby, find the elevators, press the button, get in, ride to the top.

If you are consistently stumped by a step, try breaking it up into two or three smaller steps first.

2. Step No Longer Important or Relevant

Sometimes a step is not the huge priority you think it is. As you proceed in your Do List, conditions change and better steps become apparent. Betty Lou found that she kept putting off looking for a part-time job. She found that she could get some financial aid in the form of grants, loans, and work study arrangements, which enabled her to stay on campus all day, take a heavier load, and graduate earlier.

Go over your Do List frequently and alter or delete steps that are no longer so important or relevant.

3. Problem Solving Blocked by Bigger Problem

When you are up against an important step in your Do List, you may find that old blocks to problem solving reassert themselves. You might be overwhelmed with feelings of anxiety, shame, or self-doubt. You might experience a resurgence of worries that you will anger, disappoint, or inconvenience others if you pursue your solution too vigorously. You might suffer renewed doubts about your competence or worth.

If this is the case, you need to return to the first part of this book and deal with your blocks to problem solving. Review your revised self-statements and coping plans so you can reduce the debilitating feelings to a tolerable level and proceed with the next step.

Where to Go From Here

As you start performing the first tasks on your Do List, new vistas of change and growth will open up for you. Your experiences will alter your perception of your problem and your best strategy for solving it. You will need to start evaluating your problem-solving progress and making adjustments.

After trying the first few steps of your Do List, go on to the next chapter on "Evaluation."

11

Evaluation

Evaluation is a crucial step in problem solving. This chapter is like the end of a long crocheted scarf—all the loose ends have to be turned back and woven into the fabric or else the whole thing might unravel. Evaluation is an opportunity to make sense of what you've done so far, and decide where you need to go from here. If problem solving isn't working, this chapter will help you find out why.

If you've gotten to this step, you at least possess or have begun work on a Do List. There are three possible outcomes for any Do List, and each requires a different kind of analysis:

1. You've completed most or all of your Do List, and need to evaluate how actual consequences compare to the consequences you predicted. In other words, is your problem-solving strategy working or unlikely to work?

2. You've completed some Do List steps, but have gotten bogged down.

3. You can't get started on your Do List, or you've gotten stuck on the earliest steps.

Let's start with situation 1.

When You've Completed Much or All of Your Do List

At this point it's a good idea to evaluate outcomes and compare predicted with actual consequences. The process is simple. On the Reality Checklist to follow, write each Do List step in the left-hand column. In the middle column—Predicted Consequences—list all the positive and negative outcomes you identified in Chapter 9 on "Consequences." These outcomes may be attached to a particular Do List step, or be listed as General Consequences at the bottom third of the column.

Now, in the Actual Consequences column, list every positive and negative outcome you've observed so far. Again, these outcomes may be associated with a particular Do List step, or you can list them at the bottom as General Consequences of your problem-solving strategy.

Example

Ron owns a take-out deli and wants to expand his operation to include a sit-down café. Possible strategies included building a loft space for tables, moving to a larger storefront, trying to get a license for an outdoor café, trying to take over the lease on the shoe repair shop next door, and so on. Ron's analysis of consequences made building the loft space seem like the best alternative.

After three months of Do List steps, here's what Ron wrote on his Reality Checklist. It's worth noting that Ron decided not to go forward with his plan after this analysis, and instead opted for the simpler outdoor café.

Ron's Reality Checklist

Do List Steps	Predicted Consequences	Actual Consequences
1. Get lease addendum from landlord agreeing to construction of loft.	None	Two months of idiotic negotiating; a $1,000 rent increase.
2. Hire architect, develop design for a 10 table loft.	$3,000 fee	Charged $6,000, took three months.
3. Get permit.	$250 fee	$250, but forced a redesign that cost $3,000 more in architectural fees. Reduced loft size to a point it can only carry six tables.
4. Hire contractor.	$20,000 estimated costs	$35,000 bid from contractor.
5. Close business during remodeling.	Two weeks construction; $8,000 in lost business during construction.	Estimates one-month construction. Would lose $16,000 in business.
6. Buy tables and chairs.	$3,000	$2,000
7. Hire a wait staff.	Hire minimum wage college kids, but still a significant payroll increase.	
General Consequences	Approximately $35,000 in start-up costs. Expect to increase business by 50%—more than $8,000 per month	$62,000 in start-up costs. With only six tables, business expected to increase by $5,000 or less. Unexpected rent increase reduces profit.

Now it's your turn to evaluate the specific consequences of your Do List steps, as well as overall outcomes for your problem-solving strategy. Right now, fill in the blank Reality Checklist below.

My Reality Checklist		
Do List Steps	**Predicted Consequences**	**Actual Consequences**
General Consequences		

Depending on what you discover with the Reality Checklist, you may:

- Conclude that your problem-solving strategy is a success, and move on to other problem-solving efforts.

- Conclude that your problem-solving strategy likely will be a success, but you'll continue evaluating it as you finish the last Do List steps.

- Conclude that your problem-solving strategy has more negative outcomes than predicted, and you need to return to Chapter 9 step, Consequences to select your next most likely to succeed strategy.

When You've Completed *Some* of Your Do List, But Got Bogged Down

If you've completed some Do List steps, but have lost momentum, it's time to ask yourself three key questions.

First, *are you making progress toward your goal?* If you were to rate your satisfaction from zero (unsatisfied) to 9 (extremely satisfied), how satisfied are you with the outcome so far?

A second question regards the Do List items themselves. *Are the steps of the Do List effectively organized to help you reach your goal?* In other words, are the steps too big, too small? Do they require prerequisite skills you don't have? Rate the Do List from zero (overwhelmingly difficult) to 9 (highly achievable).

And a final question, *how desirable does the goal now feel to you?* Where is it on the scale from zero (no longer meaningful or motivating) to 9 (extremely important and desirable)?

If your rating for question 1 was 4 or below, you should return to the chapters on brainstorming and consequences to reconsider the strategy you've chosen. It's possible the work on your Do List has shown that you are on the wrong track. Maybe you should choose another strategy, evaluate consequences, and develop a new Do List.

A low rating on question one or two might also suggest a re-evaluation of your Do List items. Maybe they're too daunting. Maybe the steps require too much time, energy, or skills you don't have. If this is the case, the Do List needs to be broken down into smaller, more achievable steps, or preliminary steps need to be added so you don't stumble coming out of the gate. If you want to think more specifically about the organizational problems in your current Do List, look at the Organizational Problems section in the Problem Checklist on the following page.

If your answer to question three shows that your original goal is less desirable, less motivating now, return to the "Assessment" chapter. It's time to redefine your statement of the problem and goal into something that you really want to work on.

When Your Do List Doesn't Get Done

If you can't get started on your Do List, or you've gotten stuck on the earliest steps, we recommend a quick tour of the Problem Checklist that follows.

My Problem Checklist

Check if this
is an issue.

_____ **1. Fear is influencing your ability to take action. You are afraid of:**

_____ Failing.

_____ Being embarrassed, humiliated, or shamed as you attempt to solve your problem; being exposed as a flawed and unworthy person.

_____ Something catastrophic or very dangerous happening if you continue your problem-solving efforts.

_____ Feeling guilty and wrong that attempts to solve your problem are going to hurt, disappoint, or deprive others of things they need.

_____ Being blamed and rejected by others if your problem-solving efforts conflict with their needs.

_____ Other

_____ **2. Organizational problems are limiting your ability to take action.**

_____ You haven't scheduled particular times to work on your Do List.

_____ You have no system for remembering your Do List commitments (i.e., writing them in an appointment book).

_____ You have no convenient work space to complete your Do List commitments.

_____ Individual steps in your Do List are too big and overwhelming.

_____ You get distracted from working consistently on one step, perhaps trying to work on multiple steps at once or branching off into unrelated tasks.

_____ You put off unpleasant, but high priority Do List items, while focusing on more enjoyable, low priority Do List tasks.

_____ **3. Procrastination due to self-deceit.**

_____ You put the Do List off, convincing yourself that you'll work quickly and efficiently later on.

_____ When it's time to work on the Do List, you begin thinking that perhaps the goal or problem isn't all that important, or you don't really need to solve it.

_____ You tell yourself that you need more pleasure and fun in your life, not to be working on goals all the time.

_____ You convince yourself that some of the Do List steps aren't necessary.

_____ You convince yourself that it's okay to put off solving the problem. After all, you've lived with it this long.

_____ Other

_____ **4. Motivation problems are limiting your ability to take action.**

      _____ You don't schedule rewards for finishing Do List commitments.

      _____ You don't make a daily review of Do List goals, and focus instead on unrelated tasks.

      _____ You don't clearly visualize your problem-solving goals, nor hold a focused image of the positive outcomes.

      _____ You don't have Do List deadlines.

      _____ Do List steps are too difficult because you haven't broken them into smaller, achievable steps.

      _____ You haven't made a contract with a friend/family member to complete specific Do List steps.

      _____ Other

_____ **5. You lack prerequisites that are necessary to even begin problem solving.**

      _____ You are missing key skills that you need to complete Do List steps.

      _____ You need emotional support to complete specific steps.

      _____ You need information/consultation to complete specific steps.

      _____ You need agreement and cooperation from others to complete specific steps.

      _____ You lack the money or resources to complete specific steps.

      _____ You lack the time or energy to complete specific steps.

      _____ Other

How to Use Your Problem Checklist

1. Fear

If you've checked items under the category of fear, you'll have to do one of two things. The first option is to get support. You need a trusted friend or family member who can give you encouragement and emotional support as you confront difficult Do List steps. Make a written contract with this person that you'll complete the step by a certain date, and that your support person will check in with you regularly to monitor your progress.

If that doesn't work, you'll need to look at how your core beliefs may be increasing your fears. And take some time to work directly on them. If you checked that you're afraid of failing, return now to Chapter 2 on "The Core Belief of Competence," and work through the exercises designed to help you overcome beliefs that you can't succeed.

A check that you're afraid of being embarrassed and humiliated in the course of problem-solving efforts should send you to Chapter 3 on "The Core Belief of Worth." There you'll find exercises to help you understand the influence of this core belief. You'll also learn strategies to help you deal with feelings of shame and alter patterns of negative thinking.

A check on the item that something catastrophic or very dangerous will happen should send you to Chapter 4 on "The Core Belief of Safety." There you will learn new coping skills both to change your thinking and better manage your fear.

If you checked that you're afraid of feeling guilty and wrong, turn to Chapter 5 on "The Core Belief of Primacy." In that chapter is a series of exercises to help you understand and overcome the belief that your needs are less important than the needs of others. If you checked that you're afraid of being blamed and rejected, you should also go to Chapter 5.

2. Organizational Problems

The items you checked under Organizational Problems will require special attention. For example, if you haven't scheduled particular times to work on your Do List, you'll need to plan them into your week. Tell friends and family that you're going to work on a Do List item at a particular time, and ask that they check in with you to learn how much you've accomplished.

If you don't have a system for remembering Do List commitments, start using your appointment book or tie Do List efforts to key events of the day or week. For example, you might work on your Do List before dinner, right after breakfast on Saturday, the hour before your favorite TV program, or right after swimming on Tuesday evening.

If you don't have an effective work space, schedule time to clean off your desk. Try to make sure your work space can remain private—at least during the time you're working on your Do List.

If Do List steps are too big, break them into bite-sized steps, and set a deadline for accomplishing the first one.

If you get distracted by other tasks, remove everything except Do List related items from your desk. Make a commitment to yourself and a trusted friend that the time committed to working on your Do List will be spent exclusively on that. When you feel bored, anxious, or uncomfortable working on a Do List item, take a five-minute tea or coffee break. *But come back to the same task.* Don't start something else. Don't slip into something easier or irrelevant.

If you're focusing on low priority Do List tasks, and putting off the unpleasant ones, you need to make a written contract with a friend or family member that includes a deadline for completing the difficult Do List step. If necessary, find a support person to be with you while completing the step. Or schedule a big reward for yourself when you finish the unpleasant task.

3. Procrastination

Procrastination, as we've defined it here, is built upon monologues of self-deception. At the moment of truth, as you contemplate taking action on a Do List item, you may engage in some distorted thinking. Here's how to cope.

Fill in the following Procrastination Worksheet to uncover and revise key distorted thoughts. In the left-hand column, write down the Do List step you've been avoiding. Then think back to the things you tell yourself that rationalize the avoidance. The five items under Procrastination in your Problem Checklist may give you some ideas. Take your time, recall as many instances as possible where you've thought about your Do List. How did you make it okay to put it off? Now list all these thoughts in the Self-Talk column of the worksheet.

The third column of the worksheet—Realities—is an opportunity to review the reasons you wanted to solve this problem in the first place. List here all the positive consequences you expect from implementing your problem-solving strategy. Now put down what you expect to happen if you remain stuck and *never* solve the problem. How would the problem, if it continued, affect you and those you care for? Will things get worse if the problem isn't fixed? Will others be seriously affected because you never took action? How will your paralysis regarding this problem affect your mood? Or your self-esteem? Finally, refute any specific lies you've told yourself in the Self-Talk column.

Example

Amy, who was stuck in her efforts to meet people, completed this worksheet.

Amy's Procrastination Worksheet

Do List Step	Self-Talk	Realities
Put an ad with my photo on a Web site for dating.	1. Don't bother with it now. You can do it when you have time on the weekend.	I want a partner, and I'm not going to find one unless I get out and meet people. I feel depressed and empty on the weekends; I'm conscious of time ticking away and my goal of family remains far off.
	2. This isn't going to work anyway; nobody's going to like my picture.	If I don't act, I'll feel a deep sense of loss and failure. I'll have missed one of the most important things in life.
	3. I'll just go to lectures and dances; it's better to meet people face-to-face anyway.	I want someone who cares about me, honors me, who watches my back, who helps me grow, who's ready to have fun, who's ready to pitch in and solve problems together.
	4. I've been alone a while. I don't have to solve it today.	
	5. Whatever I do, I'm still not going to meet a decent man. In my age group, they're either deeply flawed or screaming narcissists.	There are decent men—I just have to look. Putting it off won't help. I never do it on the weekend, or any other time. Avoidance is screwing my chances for a better life.

Amy used the realities she listed to confront her self-deception. She decided to read them over daily, and make a commitment to herself and to one of her close friends, that her ad would be posted on the Web site no later than Friday.

Now it's time for you to complete your own Procrastination Worksheet.

My Procrastination Worksheet

Do List Step	Self-Talk	Realities

4. Motivation Problems

The items you checked under Motivation also contain a built-in coping plan. If you haven't scheduled rewards for completed Do List items, set it up now. Rent a video to watch *after* finishing your Do List work. Arrange dinner at a great restaurant *after* completing a Do List step. Order yourself that plaid hunting jacket when you've gotten through a difficult item.

If you aren't making a daily review of Do List goals, start doing it now. Visualize how your life will look when you've solved the problem; see an image of each positive outcome. Visualization is serious stuff—studies show it can significantly bolster motivation by keeping you keenly aware of *why* you are working toward a goal.

Make sure each Do List item has a deadline. If you have trouble keeping deadlines, make a written contract with a trusted friend or family member about when you'll finish a specific Do List task. Be certain that you write into the contract the expectation that they will check in with you to monitor your progress.

If you have Do List items that are overwhelmingly difficult or too complex, break them into sub-steps, and set a deadline for completing the first one.

What happens if you've done all of the above and motivation remains a problem? We suggest you consider an alternative solution—probably the runner-up choice in Chapter 9 on "Consequences." Or go back to more brainstorming. It's also possible that your feelings about the problem itself have changed. Perhaps it no longer bothers you as much. Or another problem now looms that is a higher priority. In this event, return to Chapter 7 on "Assessment" to see if you need to set a new goal.

5. Prerequisites

If missing prerequisites are blocking your Do List efforts, you'll need to revise your list. Include steps at the beginning to acquire prerequisite skills, support, information consulting, help from others, more time and energy, and so on. Because missing prerequisites can be a problem of its own, you may need to do some brainstorming and select a specific strategy to deal with it.

Don't Give Up

If you're stuck, don't give up. There is a way out of any problem. Just work the five steps. Keep visualizing your goal; keep seeing all the good that will come when the problem is gone. Central to your success in problem solving is believing you can do it—and persisting. As Napoleon once said, "Victory belongs to the most persevering."

Bibliography

D'Zurilla, T. J., and M. R. Goldfried. 1971. Problem solving and behavior modification. *Journal of Abnormal Psychology* 78:107-126.

McKay, M., and P. Fanning. 1991. *Prisoners of Belief: Exposing & Changing Beliefs That Control Your Life*. Oakland, Calif.: New Harbinger Publications.

————. 2001. *Self-Esteem*. Oakland, Calif.: New Harbinger Publications.

McKay, M., M. Davis, and P. Fanning. 1997. *Thoughts & Feelings: Taking Control of Your Moods and Your Life*. Oakland, Calif.: New Harbinger Publications.

Meichenbaum, D. 1977. *Cognitive-Behavior Modification: An Integrative Approach*. Buffalo, N.Y.: Plenum.

Osborn, Alex F. 1993. *Applied Imagination: Principles and Procedures of Creative Problem Solving*. 3d, rev. ed. New York: Creative Education Foundation.

Sperry, R. W. 1961. Cerebral organization and behavior. *Science* 133:1749-1757.

Sperry, R. W., M. S. Gazzaniga, and J. E. Bogen. 1961. Interhemispheric relationships: the neocortical commissures; syndromes of hemisphere disconnection. *Handbook Clinical Neurology* 4:273-290.

Sperry, R. W. 1974. Lateral specialization in the surgically separated hemispheres. *Neurosciences Third Study Program* 3:5-19.

Young, J. E. 1999. *Cognitive Therapy for Personality Disorders: A Schema-Focused Approach.* 1Sarasota, Fla.: Professional Resource Exchange.

Patrick Fanning is a professional writer in the mental health field. He is the author of *Visualization for Change* and *Lifetime Weight Control* and coauthor of nine self-help books.

Matthew McKay, Ph.D., is the clinical director of Haight-Ashbury Psychological Services in San Francisco. McKay is the coauthor of twenty popular books, including *The Relaxation & Stress Reduction Workbook, Self-Esteem, When Anger Hurts, Prisoners of Belief,* and several professional titles.

Additional books written by the authors include *The Addiction Workbook, Self-Esteem Companion, Thoughts & Feelings, When Anger Hurts Your Kids,* and *Couple Skills,* all New Harbinger classics.

Some Other
New Harbinger Titles

The Stop Walking on Eggshells Workbook, Item SWEW $18.95

Conquer Your Critical Inner Voice, Item CYIC $15.95

The PTSD Workbook, Item PWK $17.95

Hypnotize Yourself Out of Pain Now!, Item HYOP $14.95

The Depression Workbook, 2nd edition, Item DWR2 $19.95

Beating the Senior Blues, Item YCBS $17.95

Shared Confinement, Item SDCF $15.95

Handbook of Clinical Psychopharmacology for Therpists, 3rd edition, Item HCP3 $55.95

Getting Your Life Back Together When You Have Schizophrenia, Item GYLB $14.95

Do-It-Yourself Eye Movement Technique for Emotional Healing, Item DIYE $13.95

Stop the Anger Now, Item SAGN $17.95

The Self-Esteem Workbook, Item SEWB $18.95

The Habit Change Workbook, Item HBCW $19.95

The Memory Workbook, Item MMWB $18.95

The Anxiety & Phobia Workbook, 3rd edition, Item PHO3 $19.95

Beyond Anxiety & Phobia, Item BYAP $19.95

The Self-Nourishment Companion, Item SNC $10.95

The Healing Sorrow Workbook, Item HSW $17.95

The Daily Relaxer, Item DALY $12.95

Stop Controlling Me!, Item SCM $13.95

The Anger Control Workbook, Item ACWB $17.95

Flying without Fear, Item FLY $14.95

The Shyness & Social Anxiety Workbook, Item SHYW $16.95

The Relaxation & Stress Reduction Workbook, 5th edition, Item RS5 $19.95

Energy Tapping, Item ETAP $15.95

Stop Walking on Eggshells, Item WOE $15.95

Angry All the Time, Item ALL 13.95

Call **toll free, 1-800-748-6273,** or log on to our online bookstore at **www.newharbinger.com** to order. Have your Visa or Mastercard number ready. Or send a check for the titles you want to New Harbinger Publications, Inc., 5674 Shattuck Ave., Oakland, CA 94609. Include $4.50 for the first book and 75¢ for each additional book, to cover shipping and handling. (California residents please include appropriate sales tax.) Allow two to five weeks for delivery.

Prices subject to change without notice.